SMALL BATCH COOKIES

Edd Kimber

First published in Great Britain in 2024
by Kyle Books, an imprint of Octopus Publishing
Group Limited
Carmelite House
50 Victoria Embankment
London EC4Y 0DZ

An Hachette UK Company
www.hachette.co.uk

978 1 80419 18 59

Distributed in the US by Hachette Book Group,
1290 Avenue of the Americas, 4th and 5th Floors,
New York, NY 10104

Distributed in Canada by Canadian Manda Group,
664 Annette St., Toronto, Ontario, Canada M6S 2C8

Publishing Director: Judith Hannam
Publisher: Joanna Copestick
Editor: Isabel Jessop
Art Director: Nicky Collings
Photography & Food Styling: Edd Kimber
Production: Katherine Hockley

Printed and bound in China

10 9 8 7 6 5 4 3 2 1

MIX
Paper | Supporting
responsible forestry
FSC® C008047

SMALL BATCH COOKIES

Edd Kimber
@THEBOYWHOBAKES

PHOTOGRAPHY BY EDD KIMBER

KYLE BOOKS

INTRODUCTION

If the adage that good things come in small packages is true, this book of cookies is the ultimate small package – a tribute to chocolate chip cookies, a declaration of love to oatmeal raisin, a nostalgic salute to shortbread. Cookies may be small but my love for them is mighty. If, for some unthinkably tragic reason, I was forced to make and enjoy only one type of baked good, the choice would be easy: cookies. They are the perfect bake, capable of any conceivable flavour combination and texture. They're nostalgic, quick and easy to make, and need very little equipment. The king of the cookie world, the chocolate chip cookie, is the perfect example of why I love these fabulous little treats. A fresh-from-the-oven, still slightly warm, chocolate chip cookie gives you a crisp edge, a soft and chewy centre, notes of toffee from brown sugar, and plenty of melted chocolate in every bite. There is nothing better.

But what exactly is a cookie? It may sound ridiculous, but trying to pin down a clear definition on which we can all agree is not as easy as you might think. In the UK a cookie is seen mainly as something that resembles an American chocolate chip cookie (technically classified as a drop cookie), and everything else is a biscuit. In the US, however, cookie is much more all-encompassing: an Oreo is a cookie (a biscuit if you're British) and you can even stretch the definition to include brownies and blondies, categorizing them as bar cookies. As the world has become smaller, the term has become muddled, stretched and transformed. The French did not call anything a cookie until relatively recently – they have *biscuits*, *sablés* and *gâteaux secs* (dry cakes) but have now also adopted 'le cookie', meaning different things depending on the context. This book will therefore be a broad church and take an international approach: cookies are individually baked small treats, which are generally flat and sweet. They can be cakey, chewy, crisp or crunchy and they can be made like a shortbread or a chocolate chip cookie.

Why small batch? Is greed an acceptable answer? Can I say it's because I want to have my cake (cookies) and eat them? I want to be able to make what I'm craving and not have to make a huge batch, resulting in leftovers. There are plenty of times I bake to share with large groups – for birthdays, for big celebrations. But what about the small celebrations, the 'I survived another week' celebration that deserves a little treat? Not only do small batch recipes fit into our lives, when big elaborate baking does not, but they are also a great way to use up leftover ingredients – the last bit of cream cheese to make a filling, the egg yolks that would otherwise be thrown out. Small batch baking is also inherently cheaper and less wasteful. However, as I know I'll be asked, all recipes can be doubled without issue!

MY PERFECT COOKIE MANIFESTO

I don't think you'll find many people more obsessed with cookies than I am. My freezer is regularly stocked with balls of multiple cookie doughs, ready to be baked at a moment's notice. A cookie is my comfort bake, my cheeky treat, my idea of heaven. I will take them sweet, savoury, a combo of the two, in all sizes, shapes and styles. I simply love cookies. So, I am also very picky when it comes to making the perfect cookie. After decades of cookie baking and a lifetime of cookie eating experience, this is my manifesto – my thoughts on making the most delicious cookies.

SHAPE

Does a cookie need to perfectly round? Of course not. Does it satisfy my brain and make for exceedingly pleasing cookies when they are? Yes, absolutely. I can't help it, round cookies look better to me, more delicious, more enticing. I am sure many of you will scoff at the idea of manhandling the cookies as they come out of the oven, turning their slightly irregular shape into something perfectly round, but I can't and won't be stopped. This isn't to say that you need to – I know this is silly, and you should take these recipes and follow your own path, but should you have a brain like mine, here is what to do.

Shaping

The first step for making a perfectly round cookie is to start with a ball of cookie dough. This can be achieved by using a cookie scoop, old-fashioned mechanical ice-cream scoops that are perfect for portioning out equal balls of cookie dough. You can also scoop the dough with spoons, then roll it in your hands, fashioning neat round balls. Simply put, round balls of cookie dough turn into round cookies.

Scooting

When a cookie comes out of the oven, it is soft and, importantly, still pliable. If you scoot a cookie cutter, one slightly larger than the cookie you are working with, around the outside of the cookie, it will neatly round the edges, turning what was once an irregular cookie into something perfectly round.

WEIGHTS AND SCALES

Baking by weight is better. I have heard all the arguments in the world as to why cups are more convenient, but none of them hold water with me. Scales are more efficient, create less washing up and most importantly mean there is much less wiggle room when it comes to replicating a recipe. If I call for 125g of flour, that is translated as 1 cup, but that is entirely dependent on how you measure a cup of flour – it is incredibly easy to over- or under-measure flour when using cups, causing issues with your baking. When scales are used, 125g of flour is always 125g of flour. Yes,

there are cup conversions included in this book, but I implore you to bake by weight. These recipes were developed using the metric system and if you switch to using scales you'll soon see the light and be converted to baking with scales – it is the only true way.

INGREDIENTS

Cookies are simple things, made with little effort and very few ingredients. Because of their simplicity, it is important to use good ingredients, but mainly it is about using ingredients you love. When you add chunks of chocolate to a cookie dough, that flavour won't magically transform in the oven, so use something you already enjoy the taste of, because it's about to be the hero of your cookie. Similarly, butter is a significant building block of a cookie and its flavour is going to be key to the perfect bite. Here in the UK, and in Europe more broadly, we are incredibly lucky that our dairy is of great quality and good butter is very easy to come by – even standard supermarket butter will make a great cookie. Am I saying you need to go and spend a small fortune on hand-churned butter from some French mountainside? No, not at all, but a quality butter can really make your cookie shine.

SALT

You would never guess how many emails I have received, over the years, from people horrified at my use of salt, not because I use too much, because they simply HATE that a cookie has salt sprinkled on the outside. If you are one of these people, I understand your feelings, but let me explain. Cookies have lots of sugar and the salt in the dough is to balance this and, as in regular cooking, to help season the recipe, to bring out all of the flavours and to make something delicious. A cookie without salt can taste one dimensional, lacking depth. The salt on the outside of a cookie does the same job but, importantly, it also adds little pops of saltiness which, to me, are magic. They make a cookie sparkle, and give a more pronounced sweet and salty result. This works particularly well with cookies that include chocolate or anything caramel-esque. It also works wonderfully where butter is the main flavour, but:

IF THE SALT SPRINKLED ON TOP OF A COOKIE OFFENDS YOU, I GIVE YOU PERMISSION TO LEAVE IT OFF.

TO CREAM OR NOT TO CREAM

The base of most cookies is a mingling of butter and sugar together, and how that marriage is achieved can happen one of two ways: by creaming the ingredients together until light and fluffy, or melting the butter and simply mixing it together with the sugar using a spatula. While these methods can be used interchangeably, the method used will have a pronounced effect on the end texture. Creaming adds lots of air to the butter, creating a cookie that is lighter, which, depending on the other ingredients and the ratio at which they are used, can create a crumblier shortbread, a thicker, cakier drop cookie, a lighter and fluffier cake-based cookie. When the ingredients are combined after the butter is melted, the dough lacks that added air, which can lead to denser textures, chewier textures. Knowing this, you can choose your method and adapt recipes to alter their end texture.

FUN!

The above might make it seem like I take the topic of cookies entirely too seriously, and you're probably right, but what I never forget is that at their heart, cookies, like all baking really, are meant to be joyous. Baking is, I can confidently say, entirely superfluous, well at least baking of the sweet variety. We don't need cookies or cakes to survive, they're not the food that sustains us, and because of this baking should be the thing that brings us joy, which puts a smile on our faces. Baking is a bonus, a treat, a celebration. Is a salad going to turn around a rubbish day? Probably not. But you know what will? A cookie, of course.

THE BORING BUT IMPORTANT BIT

Please Do Not Skip

I know these parts of cookbooks can be boring and it's tempting to jump ahead to the recipes, to get straight to the fun part, but just as reading a recipe through a couple times before you attempt it is important, reading these few pages can be an incredibly useful primer on the recipes that follow. My aim is to arm you with as much useful instruction and advice as possible, so that you can easily recreate all of the wonderful recipes in this book without stress or worry. As this book is likely to be read in multiple countries around the world, it is important to look at ingredients and equipment because what is available in each country can vary significantly, and the details provided here can help you make the right choice when looking for what's best to use.

Ingredients

FLOUR

Coupled with using the correct egg size, your choice of flour will have the most impact when replicating these recipes at home, wherever you are in the world. Most recipes in this book use plain flour, a white wheat flour with a moderate protein content. In the US, for example, the closest equivalent to British plain flour is all-purpose flour, but to ensure the closest possible match, it's a little more complicated than a simple switch. All flours have a different rate of absorption – the amount of moisture they can soak up – and if you use something that differs significantly from what I use, you may find your cookies spread more or less than is shown in the accompanying image of said cookie. This absorption rate is unfortunately never listed on the side of a flour sack but there is a proxy, something to give you a bit of guidance: the protein content. Protein is one of the elements that affects absorption: the higher the protein content, the higher the rate of absorption. Because of this, it is generally advised that instead of looking at the type of the flour, you look at the protein content. In the UK, plain flour tends to have a protein content of around 9–10%. In the US, for example, the protein content in all-purpose flour tends to average higher because some brands have significantly higher protein content, almost 12%. So, yes, you can use all-purpose flour, but look for one that has a similar level of protein as the flours in the UK. It is also important to use unbleached flour, as the flour I use here in the UK is unbleached and the bleaching process makes flour more absorbent.

EGGS

If you live outside the UK or Europe, this one bit of information could prove invaluable. I call for large eggs, which in the UK, Europe and Australia means the same thing as the sizes are the same in all of these countries. Elsewhere this can differ, by quite a significant amount, so you need to use the egg size that most closely resembles a UK large egg. In the US, for example, this would be an extra-large egg and the same goes for Canada. The labelling of egg sizes is generally controlled countrywide, so this is normally very easy to find with a quick google search. In the UK, a large egg weighs between 63–73g (2¼–2½oz), still in the shell.

BUTTER

Butter is a foundational ingredient when it comes to cookies, so for clarity I should specify that all recipes were tested using standard supermarket unsalted butter, which in the UK and Europe means a standardized fat content of 82%. Outside of Europe, this style of butter is often sold as European-style but just look for something similar, an unsalted butter with around 82% fat content. Unsalted butter is called for simply because it is easier to control the salt level in a recipe when you know how much salt is in the butter: zero. The level of salt in salted butter will vary, so it easier to use butter without any added to standardize the recipe.

GLUTEN-FREE INGREDIENTS

Because there are multiple brands of gluten-free flour, which can vary significantly, brand by brand and country by country, I decided to skip these flours altogether and make my gluten-free recipes utilising naturally gluten-free grains like oat flour and buckwheat flour, and even just good old ground almonds (almond meal). This book includes many recipes that use oats, and while oats are naturally gluten-free, it is important, if baking for someone with an allergy, that the oats you are using are classified as gluten-free as not all are (due to cross-contamination). The same goes for baking powder. All the gluten-free recipes in this book are marked with a GF symbol.

VEGAN INGREDIENTS

For the vegan recipes in this book (all marked with a V symbol), I found, through lots of experimentation and many batches of cookies, that egg alternatives such as flax or psyllium husk were entirely superfluous for small batch cookies. In most cases, the egg has been easily replaced with plant-based milk with stellar results. To replace the butter, a simple swap to vegan butter was all that was required. When shopping for a vegan butter, look for a version sold as a block, not something spreadable. If you are looking at the non-vegan recipes in the book and wondering if they can be made vegan, look for recipes without any egg as these recipes will generally veganize without worry by simply switching the dairy ingredients for vegan alternatives. For those recipes which contain egg, you can normally switch this out for a plant-based milk, but a little experimentation would be needed to get the correct ratio. For non-vegan bakers, if you spot a vegan recipe you'd like to un-veganize, to make it with the ingredients you have on hand, you can simply swap the vegan ingredients for the dairy versions. When shopping for vegan ingredients, you may be surprised that not all sugar is vegan, as some producers use bone char in the process of refining sugar. In the UK this isn't a problem as the main producers eliminated this practice many years ago. In the US, look for organic sugar as USDA-certified organic sugars cannot use this process either. In regard to chocolate I mainly use dark (semisweet or bittersweet) chocolate in vegan baking because it is naturally vegan, but even so, it is still worth checking the packaging in case it can't be classed as vegan due to additives or cross-contamination.

CHOCOLATE

If you have read any of my other books, you'll notice that when chocolate is called for, I generally give a percentage of cocoa solids that the chocolate should include. In this book this is almost entirely absent, not because it isn't important, but because in this book the chocolate is mainly mixed into the cookie dough at the end, not used in the dough itself. Because chocolate isn't used as a foundational ingredient, you have more leeway in what you use; the choice is yours because it's more about preference. As a general guide, I tend to use a dark chocolate with around 65–70% cocoa solids and milk chocolate with 35–40% cocoa solids, but this is my personal taste and what I think works well in baking, adding the right amount of flavour without too much additional sweetness. Remember, the most important thing when choosing chocolate for your cookies is to use one that you love the taste of – that way you'll love the finished cookie.

SUGAR

The most commonly used sugars in this book are caster sugar and light brown sugar. Caster sugar – sometimes also sold as baker's, or superfine, sugar – is a finely ground white sugar; it has a fine granulated texture. In countries where this sugar doesn't exist, the closest equivalent is generally called granulated sugar and can be used as a 1:1 alternative. You can also make caster sugar at home by simply blitzing granulated sugar in a food processor for a few seconds. For light brown sugar, I like to use an unrefined muscovado sugar, as it has a higher molasses content and therefore a greater depth of flavour. If you are looking at options for brown sugar and see the terms 'unrefined' or 'organic', these are normally signs that the sugar will have a higher level of molasses and have a robust flavour. I often use demerara sugar for a final flourish, to add texture. You can substitute this with turbinado sugar if demerara is unavailable.

SYRUPS

In a handful of recipes, I call for both golden syrup and black treacle, two very classic British ingredients for baking that don't have wide distribution outside of Commonwealth countries. Golden syrup can often be found in the international aisle of supermarkets and can also be replaced by honey. I avoid using corn syrup, simply as it has zero flavour. Black treacle is very similar to molasses, so if treacle is unavailable, then using molasses is the closest substitute. Both of these ingredients are also very easy to buy online and last an incredibly long time, so having some in your cupboards for when you are baking British recipes is an easy solution.

PEANUT BUTTER

Peanut butter is one of my all-time favourite ingredients to use in baking, but choosing the style you use is important, as they are not all made in the same way. Many 'natural' peanut butters split when left to sit and this lack of emulsion can affect how a cookie bakes. I prefer to use a commercial smooth peanut butter, like Skippy, for consistent results.

OATS

Oats are a frequently used ingredient in this book, but choosing the right style is important. Some recipes use traditional rolled oats and some use simple porridge oats, which are smaller and thinner, adding less texture to a recipe. When following a recipe, make sure you use the variety called for.

MALT POWDER

Malt adds a great depth of flavour to many a recipe, and while there are specialist forms of malt you can buy to bake with, I find it easiest to use a malted milk powder you can buy easily from the supermarket, such as Horlicks or Ovaltine. Just make sure the malted milk powder isn't flavoured with anything else – a classic malted milk powder is what you're looking for.

VANILLA

When making cookies, especially small batch, I generally use either vanilla bean paste or vanilla extract. If you only have one on hand, you can substitute one for the other, but just remember that vanilla bean paste has a stronger, more concentrated flavour, so you will need to use more extract if using that, generally double the amount of paste.

COCOA POWDER

Cocoa powder can be a little confusing because there are two types, but the packaging often lacks the clarity to distinguish between them. There is Natural and Dutched, the latter being the most commonly used in baking, and what is used exclusively in this book. While the word Dutched may not appear on the packaging, you may see 'processed with an alkali', or something similar . You can also tell the difference by the colour. Natural cocoa powder has a light dusty colour, Dutched has a richer, deeper brown colour. In some recipes, I like to use black cocoa, a variety of Dutched cocoa powder with a jet black colour and an almost savoury flavour. If black cocoa is called for and you don't have any on hand, you can use regular Dutched cocoa powder in its place.

Recipe Key

GF = Gluten-free

V = Vegan

EQUIPMENT

For small batch baking you need the usual standard items, such as bowls and wire racks. However, there are a few other items that are especially helpful when baking small.

BUTTER WARMER/ MILK PAN

These two small pans are extremely useful. The butter warmer is a mini pan, about 8cm (3in) in diameter, and can be used for all manner of tasks, such as melting small amounts of chocolate and warming small amounts of leftover custards and sauces, as well as for melting butter. Milk pans are about 15cm (6in) in diameter and, apart from heating milk, are perfect for making small batches of choux pastry or sauces, or for setting up as a bain-marie (double boiler).

HAND-HELD MIXER

Stand mixers, such as KitchenAids and Kenwoods, are not designed for small batch bakes, so whipping a single egg white in one of these machines is not all that effective. However, a hand-held mixer, the type with two detachable beaters, is the perfect tool for small batch baking. It is also significantly cheaper than a stand mixer.

SMALL OFFSET SPATULAS

I recommend offset spatulas for every style of baking, but they are especially useful when baking small. They are great to use as mini sptaulas for moving cookies to wire racks, and perfect for spreading frostings or fillings.

MINI SPATULAS/ WOODEN SPOONS

My kitchen is overflowing with spatulas and wooden spoons in a wide range of sizes, but I always opt for small ones when working with small batches of ingredients, as the standard ones can be a little cumbersome.

MINI BALLOON WHISK/ SAUCE WHISK

While a big balloon whisk is a standard item in many kitchens, it may not be the most effective tool for all small batch tasks. I often find a mini balloon whisk or a small sauce whisk more effective, especially for anything prone to clumping or going lumpy.

SIX-HOLE MUFFIN TRAY

If you already have a standard 12-hole muffin tray, there is no need to buy a smaller one. However, if you're starting from scratch and storage is an issue in your kitchen, a 6-hole tray is all you'll need for small batch baking.

SMALL BAKING TRAY/ EIGHTH SHEET PAN

For most of the recipes in this book the exact size of baking tray is not important; you can use what you already have. For the smallest of recipes an eighth sheet pan – a small rimmed baking tray, which measures 23 × 15cm (9 × 6in) – is the perfect fit, great for baking off one or two cookies.

COOKIE CUTTERS

Perfect for shortbreads, sablés and all manner of recipes, a large round cookie cutter is also a great tool for scooting drop cookies back into shape while they're still warm (see page 8).

ELECTRONIC SCALES

Accuracy is always important in baking, but even more so when baking small batches, so I always advise baking by weight to ensure the correct result. The only recipe where this doesn't hold true is the Single Serve Pecan Butterscotch Cookie (page 164), where measuring spoons are used instead. Electronic scales are cheap and easy to use, and because they can be zeroed between each weighed ingredient, they also mean less washing up.

AIR FRYERS

The recipes in this book were tested for traditional home ovens but with the rise in popularity of air fryers, it is worth noting many of the recipes will work perfectly made in an air fryer. A little experimentation would be needed to get the correct bake temperature and time but the best general advice I can give you is to lower the temperature and reduce the bake time: start with a reduction of about 20ºC (25ºF) and cut a third of the bake time.

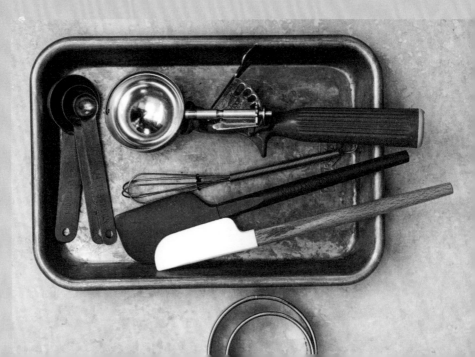

SOFT & SUMPTUOUS

Blueberry Muffin Top Cookies

MAKES 6

Can we all agree the best part of a blueberry muffin is the muffin top? With its mixture of textures, the crisp edge and the soft centre, it almost sounds like a cookie, doesn't it? These cookies are part cake, part cookie, soft and dense and with all the flavour of your favourite muffin, streusel topping included.

115g (4oz/1 stick) unsalted butter, at room temperature

125g (4½oz/½ cup + 2 tablespoons) caster (superfine or granulated) sugar

1 large egg

1 teaspoon vanilla extract

185g (6½oz/1½ cups) plain (all-purpose) flour

2 tablespoons cornflour (cornstarch)

¼ teaspoon fine sea salt

½ teaspoon baking powder

¼ teaspoon bicarbonate of soda (baking soda)

100g (3½oz/½ cup) frozen blueberries

FOR THE STREUSEL TOPPING

35g (1¼oz/4 tablespoons) plain (all-purpose) flour

25g (1oz/2 tablespoons) caster (superfine or granulated) sugar

25g (1oz/1¾ tablespoons) unsalted butter, melted

20g (¾oz/¼ cup) traditional rolled oats

Preheat the oven to 180ºC (160ºC Fan) 350ºF, Gas Mark 4 and line a large baking tray (sheet pan) with parchment paper.

For the streusel topping, mix together the flour and sugar. Pour over the melted butter and stir together with a fork until a crumbly mixture is formed. Add the oats and mix to combine, pressing into a ball of dough. Pop the streusel in the refrigerator until needed.

For the cookie dough, in a large bowl, beat together the butter and sugar until light and fluffy, about 5 minutes. Add the egg and vanilla and beat briefly to combine. Add the flour, cornflour, salt, baking powder and bicarbonate of soda and mix together until a cake-like batter is formed. Add the blueberries and mix until they are evenly distributed.

Using a 60ml (4 tablespoon/¼ cup) cookie scoop, scoop the dough onto the prepared baking tray in 6 equal rounds, leaving room for spreading. Remove the streusel mixture from the refrigerator, break into small chunks and press onto the cookies. Bake for 18–20 minutes, or until lightly browned around the edges and still a little pale in the centre. Because of the berries, the cookies may spread in a slightly erratic and irregular manner; if you want the cookies to be neat and round, use a large round cookie cutter to scoot them back into shape after roughly half the bake time has elapsed.

Remove the baking tray from the oven and allow the cookies to cool for 5 minutes before transferring to a wire rack to cool completely.

If stored in a sealed container, these cookies will keep for 2–3 days but they will soften further as they age.

NOTE I like to use frozen blueberries in this recipe as they release a little more juice as they bake, creating a more colourful and delicious-looking cookie. You can use fresh blueberries should you prefer.

Malted Black and White Cookies

MAKES 6

These NYC-style black and white cookies are one of my favourite things, so much so that I once spent days trawling the bakeries of New York trying to find the best (my favourites came from Russ & Daughters and William Greenberg Desserts). This version stays close to the classic, a soft cake-like cookie, but I add malt to the dough to add a cosy warmth, which pairs beautifully with the vanilla and chocolate icing.

85g (3oz/¾ stick) unsalted butter, at room temperature

100g (3½oz/½ cup) caster (superfine or granulated) sugar

1 large egg

½ teaspoon vanilla bean paste

¼ teaspoon fine sea salt

150g (5½oz/1 cup + 3 tablespoons) plain (all-purpose) flour

4 tablespoons malted milk powder

¼ teaspoon baking powder

¼ teaspoon bicarbonate of soda (baking soda)

60ml (4 tablespoons/¼ cup) soured cream

FOR THE ICINGS

180g (6oz/1½ cups) icing (powdered) sugar, sifted

1 tablespoon liquid glucose or corn syrup (or honey if you can't get hold of either)

½ teaspoon vanilla bean paste

2 tablespoons cocoa powder

Preheat the oven to 180°C (160°C Fan) 350°F, Gas Mark 4 and line a large baking tray (sheet pan) with parchment paper.

In a large bowl, using an electric hand mixer, beat together the butter and sugar until light and fluffy, about 5 minutes. Add the egg, vanilla and salt and mix briefly just until evenly distributed. Add the flour, malt powder, baking powder and bicarbonate of soda and mix until a batter is formed. Add the soured cream and mix briefly to combine.

Using a 60ml (4 tablespoon/¼ cup) cookie scoop, spoon the dough into 6 equal rounds on the prepared baking tray, leaving plenty of room for spreading. If your baking tray is small, you may want to use 2 trays to avoid the cookies spreading into each other as they bake.

Bake for 12–13 minutes, or until the edges are lightly browned and the centres are pale but also spring back to a light touch. Remove from the oven and set aside until fully cooled.

For the icings, mix together the icing sugar, liquid glucose, vanilla and 2 tablespoons of boiling water until smooth and lump free. Add half of the icing to a separate bowl and mix through the cocoa powder and about ½ tablespoon of boiling water. The finished icings should have the same consistency as each other – they can be adjusted with extra water to thin them out or extra icing sugar to thicken them up.

To decorate the cookies, spread the vanilla icing over the flat side of the cookies, coating just one half of each cookie. Spread the cocoa icing across the other half of each cookie and set aside until the icing has set, about 30 minutes.

If stored in a sealed container, these cookies will keep for 2–3 days.

Brown Butter Honey Cornmeal Cookies

MAKES 6

These are cookies to make on a cold, wet autumnal day when you want something warming and cosy. The brown butter, honey and cornmeal (polenta) combo gives these cookies a wonderfully deep and rich flavour, like the best cornbread but in cookie form.

75g (2½oz/⅓ cup) unsalted butter, diced

50g (1¾oz/¼ cup) caster (superfine or granulated) sugar

25g (1oz/1 heaped tablespoon) honey

1 large egg yolk

¼ teaspoon vanilla extract

75g (2½oz/½ cup + 1½ tablespoon) plain (all-purpose) flour

60g (2¼oz/⅓ cup + 1 tablespoon) fine cornmeal (polenta)

¼ teaspoon bicarbonate of soda (baking soda)

¼ teaspoon baking powder

¼ teaspoon fine sea salt

First, we need to brown the butter. Add the butter to a small saucepan and place over a medium heat. The butter will first bubble and splatter as the water content is cooked out, but once settled it will start to foam and at this point you want to watch carefully for the milk solids to turn the butter a nutty brown. Pour the butter into a bowl along with the sugar and honey, mixing together briefly to combine. Set the bowl aside to cool for 10 minutes.

Preheat the oven to 180ºC (160ºC Fan) 350ºF, Gas Mark 4 and line a large baking tray (sheet pan) with parchment paper.

Add the egg yolk and vanilla to the browned butter mixture and whisk until smooth and combined. Add the dry ingredients and mix to form a uniform cookie dough. Using a 60ml (4 tablespoon/¼ cup) cookie scoop, form the dough into 6 equal balls on the prepared baking tray.

Bake the cookies for about 12 minutes, rotating halfway through baking, until the cookies are set and the edges are lightly browned. Remove and set aside for 5 minutes before transferring to a wire rack to cool completely.

If stored in a sealed container, these cookies will keep for 2–3 days.

Soft Peanut Butter and Miso Cookies

MAKES 4

I love big soft cookies, but when it comes to peanut butter cookies, the flavour tends to dissipate when the cookies veer away from either dense or crisp territory, as the other ingredients dull the flavour of the peanut butter. To counteract this, these cookies use a little white miso to add a depth of flavour and slight savouriness, which has the effect of boosting the peanut butter flavour.

85g (3oz/¼ cup + 2 tablespoons) light brown sugar

½ teaspoon vanilla extract

50g (1¾oz/3 tablespoons + 1 teaspoon) smooth peanut butter, at room temperature

50g (1¾oz/3 tablespoons) white miso paste

50g (1¾oz/3½ tablespoons) unsalted butter, diced

1 large egg yolk

100g (3½oz/¾ cup + 1 tablespoon) plain (all-purpose) flour

½ teaspoon baking powder

¼ teaspoon bicarbonate of soda (baking soda)

Pinch of fine sea salt

50g (1¾oz/¼ cup) granulated sugar, for coating

Line a large baking tray (sheet pan) with parchment paper.

Add the sugar, vanilla, peanut butter, miso and butter to a small saucepan and place over a low heat. Stir together until fully melted, then scrape into a bowl and set aside until cooled to room temperature. Once cooled, add the egg yolk, mixing until fully combined. Add the dry ingredients and mix together, using a small spatula, until a uniform cookie dough is formed.

Using a 60ml (4 tablespoon/¼ cup) cookie scoop, or a spoon, portion out the cookie dough onto the prepared baking tray and refrigerate for 20 minutes.

Preheat the oven to 180°C (160°C Fan) 350°F, Gas Mark 4.

Once chilled, roll the scooped dough into balls and roll in a bowl the granulated sugar to coat. Place back on the baking tray and bake for about 16 minutes, rotating halfway through baking, or until the edges of the cookies are lightly browned and the centres set. Remove from the oven and allow the cookies to cool for 5 minutes before transferring to a wire rack to cool completely.

If stored in a sealed container, these cookies will keep for 2–3 days.

NOTE If you want to add more texture to these cookies, add a few tablespoons of roughly chopped salted peanuts to the dough when you mix in the flour.

Chai Pumpkin Snickerdoodles

MAKES 6

Made with a blend of spices and black tea, these masala chai-inspired cookies are an homage to one of my favourite beverages and one of my favourite cookies: masala chai and the humble snickerdoodle. If that doesn't sound autumnal enough, let's throw in some pumpkin for good measure. The combination of flavours is warm and cosy, wrapped up in a cookie with a fudgy centre and a chewy edge. A pumpkin spice latte wishes it could be this good.

115g (4oz/1 stick) unsalted butter

1 black teabag

60g (2¼oz/5 tablespoons) caster (superfine or granulated) sugar

60g (2¼oz/¼ cup + 1 teaspoon) light brown soft sugar

80g (2¾oz/⅓ cup) canned pumpkin purée

1 large egg yolk

¼ teaspoon vanilla extract

100g (3½oz/¾ cup + 1 tablespoon) plain (all-purpose) flour

½ teaspoon bicarbonate of soda (baking soda)

½ teaspoon cream of tartar

¼ teaspoon fine sea salt

½ teaspoon ground cinnamon

¼ teaspoon ground cardamom

¼ teaspoon ground ginger

¼ teaspoon freshly grated nutmeg

FOR THE SPICED SUGAR COATING

50g (1¾oz/¼ cup) granulated sugar

½ teaspoon ground cinnamon

¼ teaspoon ground cardamom

¼ teaspoon ground ginger

¼ teaspoon freshly grated nutmeg

Preheat the oven to 180ºC (160ºC Fan) 350ºF, Gas Mark 4 and line a baking tray (sheet pan) with parchment paper.

Add the butter to a small saucepan and place over a medium heat. Rip open the teabag and add the tea leaves to the butter. Cook the butter until browned. As it cooks it will first splutter, as the water is cooked out, then it will then start to foam. It is at this stage you should watch for brown flecks to appear. Once nutty and brown, pour the butter into a large bowl through a fine mesh sieve to remove the tea leaves. Add the sugars to the butter and mix to combine. Set aside to cool for a couple minutes.

While the butter cools, scrape the pumpkin purée onto a couple sheets of kitchen paper towels and sandwich with a couple more sheets. Press the pumpkin into a thin flat layer, blotting as much moisture from the purée as possible.

Once the butter is no longer hot, add the pumpkin purée, egg yolk and vanilla and mix until smooth. In a separate bowl, mix together the flour, bicarbonate of soda, cream of tartar, salt and spices. Pour the flour mixture into the bowl with the butter mixture and mix together to form a cookie dough.

Divide the dough into 6 equal pieces and roll each one into a ball. Add the spices for the spiced sugar coating to a small bowl and mix together with the granulated sugar. Roll the balls of cookie dough in the spiced sugar, then place on the prepared baking tray, setting them well apart to account for spreading.

Bake for about 12 minutes, rotating halfway through baking, or until the edges are golden. Set aside to cool for 5 minutes before transferring to a wire rack to cool completely.

If stored in a sealed container, these cookies will keep for 3–4 days.

Toasted Sesame and Honey Cookies

MAKES 6

Made with a triple dose of sesame, these cookies have a warm, toasty flavour and a soft, tender texture, with a little added crunch from the generous coating of sesame seeds. If you are unsure about using sesame as the dominant flavour in a cookie, think of sesame as a cousin to peanut butter; the nuttiness works brilliantly in sweet bakes.

65g (2¼oz/¼ cup + 1 teaspoon) unsalted butter, diced and at room temperature

2 teaspoons toasted sesame oil

50g (1¾oz/scant ¼ cup) light brown sugar

50g (1¾oz/2½ tablespoons) honey

50g (1¾oz/3 tablespoons + 1 teaspoon) tahini

1 large egg yolk

1 tablespoon whole milk

¼ teaspoon vanilla extract

65g (2¼oz/½ cup) plain (all-purpose) flour

65g (2¼oz/½ cup) strong white bread flour

¼ teaspoon bicarbonate of soda (baking soda)

¼ teaspoon baking powder

¼ teaspoon fine sea salt

Toasted black and white sesame seeds, for coating

Add the butter to a small saucepan, place over a medium heat and cook until browned. The butter will first bubble and splatter as the water content is cooked out, but once settled it will start to foam and at this point you want to watch carefully for the milk solids to turn the butter a nutty brown. As the butter browns, add the oil, sugar, honey and tahini to a large bowl and whisk to form a thick paste. Pour the browned butter into the sugar mixture and whisk to combine. Allow to cool for a couple minutes, then add the egg yolk, milk and vanilla and whisk until smooth and fully combined.

In a separate bowl, whisk together the flours, bicarbonate of soda, baking powder and salt. Add the dry ingredients to the butter mixture and mix with a spatula to form a dough.

When combined, the cookie dough will initially look like a batter but as it sits the mixture will thicken. To aid this, refrigerate the dough for 30 minutes before using.

Preheat the oven to 180°C (160°C Fan) 350°F, Gas Mark 4 and line a large baking tray (sheet pan) with parchment paper. Line a plate with a mixture of black and white sesame seeds.

Remove the cookie dough from the refrigerator and divide into 6 equal pieces. Roll each piece of dough into a ball, then roll in the sesame seeds, ensuring the whole cookie is covered. Place the cookies on the baking tray, setting them well apart to allow for spreading.

Bake the cookies for about 16 minutes, rotating halfway through baking, until the edges are golden and the centres still a little pale. Remove from the oven and allow to cool for 5 minutes before transferring to a wire rack to cool completely.

If stored in a sealed container, these cookies will keep for 3–4 days.

New York Oatmeal Raisin Cookies

MAKES 4

Over the last ten years, the popularity of super-sized, extremely chunky cookies has been steadily growing, largely in part to the success of Levain Bakery, in New York's Upper West Side. Their cookies are as thick as they come, and while the chocolate walnut version is the most popular I, for one, think the oatmeal raisin version reigns supreme. This, therefore, is my tribute to the NYC cookie.

100g (3½oz/¾ cup) raisins

60g (2¼oz/¼ cup) unsalted butter, at room temperature

60g (2¼oz/heaped ¼ cup) light brown sugar

30g (1oz/2½ tablespoons) caster (superfine or granulated) sugar

1 teaspoon vanilla extract

1 large egg, lightly beaten

150g (5½oz/1 cup + 3 tablespoons) plain (all-purpose) flour

2 tablespoons malted milk powder

¾ teaspoon baking powder

½ teaspoon bicarbonate of soda (baking soda)

½ teaspoon fine sea salt

100g (3½oz/1¼ cups) traditional rolled oats

Before you start the recipe, pour the raisins into a small heatproof bowl and cover with boiling water. Set aside for 30 minutes before draining away any excess water. This step keeps the raisins nice and plump and prevents them burning when on the outside of the cookies.

In a large bowl, using an electric hand mixer, beat together the butter and sugars for 2 minutes until a smooth paste is formed. We are not looking for a light and airy mixture, this should still be very dense in texture. Add the vanilla and egg and mix, on slow speed, just briefly to combine. We don't want to whip in any air, so keep this mixing as brief as possible. In another bowl, mix together the remaining ingredients. Add the dry ingredients to the butter mixture and mix until a shaggy dough is formed. Add the raisins and mix just until evenly distributed throughout the dough.

Cover the bowl and rest the dough in the refrigerator for at least 4 hours. Resting like this helps to hydrate the flour, which in turn prevents the cookies from spreading too much, leaving us with beautifully chunky cookies.

Preheat the oven to 180ºC (160ºC Fan) 350ºF, Gas Mark 4 and line a baking tray (sheet pan) with parchment paper. Divide the cookie dough into 4 pieces, roughly shaping each one into a ball. Place on the prepared baking tray and bake for about 18 minutes, rotating halfway through baking, or until very lightly browned around the edges but still pale in the centres. Remove from the oven and set aside for 5 minutes before transferring to a wire rack to cool completely.

If stored in a sealed container, these cookies will keep for 3–4 days.

Stamped Lebkuchen (V GF)

MAKES 6

It isn't Christmas, as far as I am concerned, without a deeply spiced cookie or two. There is no cookie that fits that warming, comforting bill better than the German lebkuchen; they are packed full of spices and will warm you up on the coldest of nights. This gluten-free and vegan version is deeply spiced and made with buckwheat flour for an almost earthy flavour.

25g (1oz/2 tablespoons) dark brown sugar

40g (1½oz/⅛ cup) black treacle (molasses)

1 tablespoon soy milk (or any other plant-based milk)

80g (2¾oz/⅔ cup) wholemeal buckwheat flour

¼ teaspoon ground cinnamon

¼ teaspoon ground ginger

Pinch of freshly grated nutmeg

Pinch of ground cloves

Pinch of freshly ground black pepper

⅛ teaspoon baking powder

⅛ teaspoon bicarbonate of soda (baking soda)

⅛ teaspoon fine sea salt

FOR THE LEMON GLAZE

2 teaspoons lemon juice

40g (1½oz/⅓ cup) icing (powdered) sugar, sifted

Very small pinch of fine sea salt

Add the brown sugar, treacle and milk to a small saucepan and, over a low heat, warm through, stirring occasionally, until everything is smooth and combined. Meanwhile, in a mixing bowl, whisk together the remaining ingredients.

Pour the treacle mixture into the bowl with the flour mixture and stir together, using either a sturdy spatula or a wooden spoon, to form a dough. Cover the bowl and refrigerate for at least 1 hour, or until the dough is firm.

Preheat the oven to 180°C (160°C Fan) 350°F, Gas Mark 4 and line a baking tray (sheet pan) with parchment paper.

Divide the cookie dough into 6 equal pieces and roll each one into a ball. You can bake these cookies a number of different ways. For the decorative finish I have used, roll the balls in caster sugar and use decorative cookie stamps to flatten into discs, roughly 5–6cm (2–2½in) in diameter. You can skip the sugar and decorative finish and simply flatten the cookies with your hands. Finally, you can skip the flattening altogether and simply bake as balls of cookie dough – they'll flatten slightly as they bake for a squatter, more rounded version. Place your cookies on the prepared baking tray. Bake for 10–12 minutes, or until the edges are golden brown. Remove and set aside until fully cooled before glazing.

For the glaze, simply mix together the lemon juice and icing sugar, then add the salt. Dip the cookies into the glaze, then return to the baking tray and allow the glaze to set.

If stored in a sealed container, these cookies will keep for at least a week.

Apple Cider Doughnut Cookies (V)

MAKES 6

Over the years I have spent a lot of time in New York and, to me, there is no better time to visit than the autumn, especially around Halloween, when the city feels like a film set. It is a picture-perfect, almost cliché, dose of cosiness, with pumpkins everywhere and a city bedecked in autumnal colours. In those moments, there is nothing better than enjoying an apple cider doughnut from the farmers' market, a cake doughnut made with apple cider and coated in a warming spice sugar. This recipe is an attempt to recreate that feeling in a simple cookie.

240ml (8½fl oz/1 cup) unfiltered apple juice (apple cider in the US, see Note)

60g (2¼oz/¼ cup) unsalted vegan block butter, at room temperature

70g (2½oz/⅓ cup) light brown sugar

¼ teaspoon vanilla bean paste

150g (5½oz/1 cup + 3 tablespoons) plain (all-purpose) flour

¼ teaspoon bicarbonate of soda (baking soda)

¼ teaspoon fine sea salt

FOR THE COATING

50g (1¾oz/¼ cup) granulated sugar

2 teaspoons ground cinnamon

20g (¾oz/1 tablespoon + 1 teaspoon) unsalted vegan block butter, melted

Before you make the cookie dough, you need to reduce the apple juice to concentrate its flavour. Pour the apple juice into a small saucepan and place it over a medium heat. Cook until the juice is reduced and measures just 60ml (4 tablespoons/¼ cup). Pour into a jug and set aside to cool to room temperature.

Preheat the oven to 180°C (160°C Fan) 350°F, Gas Mark 4 and line a baking tray (sheet pan) with parchment paper.

Add the vegan butter, sugar and vanilla to a large bowl and, using an electric hand mixer, beat together until light and fluffy, about 5 minutes. Add the reduced apple juice, a little at a time, beating until fully combined before adding more. If you add the apple juice too quickly it will split the butter, so go slowly. Add the flour, bicarbonate of soda and salt and mix to form a soft cookie dough.

Using a 60ml (4 tablespoon/¼ cup) cookie scoop, divide the dough into 6 cookies and set on the prepared baking tray, 5cm (2in) apart to account for spreading. Bake for 16–17 minutes, or until the edges of the cookies are starting to brown. Remove and set aside to cool for 10 minutes.

Mix together the sugar and cinnamon for the coating. Brush the cookies with a little of the melted vegan butter, then dip into the spiced sugar, coating the cookies like you would a freshly fried doughnut.

If stored in a sealed container, these cookies will keep for 2–3 days.

NOTE I should clarify that the aforementioned apple cider is not the alcoholic sort, it is the American term for unfiltered apple juice. You can use any apple juice to make this recipe but it will be best made with something similar; the less processed, the better.

Frosted London Fog Cookies

MAKES 6

A London Fog is an Earl Grey and vanilla latte, perfect for a wet and windy British day. Sometimes the drink is sweetened with a little honey and given another layer of flavour with the addition of lavender. Surprisingly, for a drink with London in its name, the drink originates from Vancouver, Canada. This cookie takes that drink and uses the component parts to make a deliciously fragrant, soft honey and Earl Grey cookie, with a light vanilla buttercream to decorate.

75g (2½oz/⅔ stick) unsalted butter, diced

50g (1¾oz/¼ cup) caster (superfine or granulated) sugar

25g (1oz/1 heaped tablespoon) honey

1 Earl Grey teabag

1 large egg yolk

¼ teaspoon vanilla extract

100g (3½oz/¾ cup + 1 tablespoon) plain (all-purpose) flour

¼ teaspoon bicarbonate of soda (baking soda)

¼ teaspoon baking powder

¼ teaspoon fine sea salt

FOR THE VANILLA BUTTERCREAM

35g (1¼oz/2½ tablespoons) unsalted butter, very soft

70g (2½oz/½ cup + 1 tablespoon) icing (powdered) sugar

Pinch of fine sea salt

½ teaspoon vanilla bean paste

1 tablespoon double (heavy) cream

Sprinkles, to decorate (optional)

Preheat the oven to 180°C (160°C Fan) 350°F, Gas Mark 4 and line a baking tray (sheet pan) with parchment paper.

Add the butter, sugar and honey to a small saucepan. Rip open the teabag and pour the tea leaves into the pan. Place the pan over a low–medium heat and cook, stirring occasionally, until the butter has melted and the mixture is smooth. Pour into a mixing bowl through a fine mesh sieve to remove the tea leaves. Leave to cool for a few minutes, then add the egg yolk and vanilla and mix until smooth and fully combined. Add the remaining dry ingredients and mix to form a batter.

Using a 30ml (2 tablespoon) cookie scoop, spoon the batter into 6 equal rounds on the prepared baking tray, setting them well apart to account for spreading. Bake for about 12 minutes, turning halfway through baking, or until the centres of the cookies spring back to a light touch. Remove and set aside to cool before frosting.

For the buttercream, add the butter to a large bowl and, using an electric mixer, beat for about 3 minutes until very soft and creamy. Add the icing sugar, in two batches, followed by the salt, and beat for at least 5 minutes, or until very pale and fluffy. Add the vanilla and cream and beat for another minute or two until fully combined.

Spread the buttercream on top of the cookies and finish with a light dusting of sprinkles if you like.

If stored in a sealed container, these cookies will keep for up to 2 days.

Triple Ginger Molasses Cookies

MAKES 6

These fabulously soft, and slightly chewy, cookies are flavoured with not one, not two, but three types of ginger for maximum spiciness. Ground ginger is supported by both freshly grated root ginger and chunks of crystallized ginger, which are also boosted further by the addition of freshly grated nutmeg and a generous sprinkle of black pepper for a well-rounded spice cookie.

65g (2¼oz/¼ cup + 1 teaspoon) unsalted vegan block butter, diced

50ml (2fl oz/3 tablespoons + 1 teaspoon) black treacle (molasses)

85g (3oz/¼ cup + 2 tablespoons) light brown sugar

1 tablespoon freshly grated root ginger

2 tablespoons soy milk (or any other plant-based milk)

80g (2¾oz/⅔ cup) plain (all-purpose) flour

80g (2¾oz/⅔ cup) strong white bread flour

½ teaspoon bicarbonate of soda (baking soda)

½ teaspoon fine sea salt

1 tablespoon ground ginger

1 teaspoon ground cinnamon

¼ teaspoon freshly grated nutmeg

¼ teaspoon freshly ground black pepper

50g (1¾oz/⅓ cup) crystallized ginger, finely chopped

Demerara (turbinado) sugar, for coating

In a large bowl, use an electric hand mixer to beat together the vegan butter, treacle and light brown sugar, beating for a couple of minutes until well combined and slightly paler in colour. Add the freshly grated ginger and mix briefly to combine. Add the milk, 1 tablespoon at a time, beating until fully combined before adding the second.

In a separate bowl, whisk together the flours, bicarbonate of soda, salt, spices and candied ginger. Add the flour mixture to the butter mixture and mix together just until a soft cookie dough is formed. Cover the dough with clingfilm (plastic wrap) or a reusable alternative and refrigerate for a couple of hours, or until fully chilled and a little firmer.

Preheat the oven to 180ºC (160ºC Fan) 350ºF, Gas Mark 4 and line a baking tray (sheet pan) with parchment paper.

Divide the dough into 6 equal pieces and roll each one into a ball. Roll each ball in demerara sugar, coating fully, then set on the prepared baking tray.

Bake for 14–15 minutes, or until the edges of the cookies are set but the centres are still a little soft. Remove and set aside for 5 minutes before transferring to a wire rack to cool completely.

If stored in a sealed container, these cookies will keep for 3–4 days.

CRISP & CRUNCHY

Crisp Lemon and Cardamom Cookies (V)

MAKES 4

As far as I am concerned cardamom is the ultimate baker's spice; it pairs so beautifully with so many different ingredients and I just love its warm, floral flavour. These vegan cookies, inspired by the tins of butter cookies you often find at Christmas, are crumbly and laced with cardamom, which is paired with a thin lemon glaze. These delicate and fragrant cookies are the perfect accompaniment to a hot cup of tea.

50g (1¾oz/3½ tablespoons) unsalted vegan block butter, softened

¼ teaspoon vanilla bean paste

Finely ground seeds from 1 cardamom pod

20g (¾oz/3 tablespoons) icing (powdered) sugar

50g (1¾oz/⅓ cup + 1 tablespoon) plain (all-purpose) flour

10g (¼oz/1 heaped tablespoon) cornflour (cornstarch)

⅛ teaspoon fine sea salt

FOR THE LEMON GLAZE

2 teaspoons lemon juice

25g (1oz/scant ¼ cup) icing (powdered) sugar, sifted

Zest of ½ lemon

Line a small baking tray (sheet pan) with parchment paper.

In a mixing bowl, beat together the vegan butter, vanilla and cardamom. Once the mixture is light and creamy, add the icing sugar and beat together for a couple of minutes until the mixture is light and pale. Add the remaining ingredients and mix to form a soft dough.

Scrape the dough into a piping bag fitted with a large star piping tip and pipe 4 cookies onto the prepared tray. I pipe large S shapes but you could pipe the cookies in any shape you prefer. The dough is soft but thick, and you'll need to apply a good amount of pressure when piping the dough. Refrigerate the finished cookies for about 30 minutes, or until firm, before baking.

Preheat the oven to 180°C (160°C Fan) 350°F, Gas Mark 4. Bake the cookies for 10–12 minutes, rotating halfway through baking, or until a pale golden colour. Remove and set aside for 5 minutes before transferring the cookies to a wire rack to cool completely.

For the glaze, mix together the lemon juice and icing sugar until a thin glaze is formed. Dip or brush the cookies with the glaze and finish by sprinkling with a little lemon zest. Set aside until the glaze sets.

If stored in a sealed container, these cookies will keep for 3–4 days but will soften a little the older they get.

Swedish Lace Cookies (GF)

MAKES 4 SANDWICH COOKIES

These crisp and lacy cookies are a cousin to British brandy snaps and brother to French Florentines but instead of using flour they go down a naturally gluten-free route and use oats and ground almonds. When baked they are light and crisp and, when sandwiched with a whisper of dark chocolate are a sophisticated two-bite treat.

15g (½oz/1 tablespoon) unsalted butter

15g (½oz/1 tablespoon) light brown sugar

1 tablespoon honey

1 tablespoon rolled oats

2 tablespoons ground almonds (almond meal)

Pinch of fine sea salt

20g (¾oz) dark chocolate, melted, for the filling

Preheat the oven to 180°C (160°C Fan) 350°F, Gas Mark 4 and line 2 baking trays (cookie sheets) with parchment paper.

Add the butter, sugar and honey to a small saucepan, place over a low heat and cook just until melted and smooth. Pour into a small bowl along with the oats, almonds and salt and mix to form a batter.

Spoon eight small dollops of the batter onto the prepared baking trays, leaving plenty of room to account for spreading. Bake for 8–10 minutes, or until the cookies are a deep golden brown and no longer look wet. If you want the cookies to look perfectly round, you can use a larger round cookie cutter to scoot them back into shape, doing so immediately after the cookies come out of the oven, before they have a chance to set. Allow the cookies to cool fully before handling.

To assemble, spoon the chocolate on the base of half the cookies, spreading to cover most of the cookie, then sandwich together with a second cookie.

These cookies need serving on the same day that they are baked.

Homemade Mint Milanos

MAKES 6 SANDWICH COOKIES

As a teenager I remember watching an American TV show (*Friends*, I think) and they mentioned the cookie Mint Milanos. For some reason I got the idea that these cookies, a supermarket staple, were the height of luxury and sophistication. On my first trip to NYC, I popped into the bodega opposite my hotel, and there in front of me was the cookie I had considered fancy, on a shelf next to a sleeping cat. The illusion was somewhat broken but I still bought a pack and proceeded to fall in love. They're light and crisp and filled with mint milk chocolate, and they're also incredibly simple to make at home.

40g (1½oz/2¾ tablespoons) unsalted butter, softened

20g (¾oz/1 tablespoon + 2 teaspoons) caster (superfine or granulated) sugar

20g (¾oz/3 tablespoons) icing (powdered) sugar

1 large egg white

55g (2oz/¼ cup + 3 tablespoons) plain (all-purpose) flour

Pinch of fine sea salt

FOR THE FILLING

50g (1¾oz) milk chocolate

⅛ teaspoon peppermint extract

Preheat the oven to 170ºC (150ºC Fan) 340ºF, Gas mark 3½ and line a baking tray (sheet pan) with parchment paper.

Add the butter and sugars to a mixing bowl and, using a wooden spoon, beat together until light and creamy, about 3 minutes. Add the egg white and beat until smooth and fully combined. Add the flour and salt and mix to form a smooth batter.

Scrape the batter into a piping bag fitted with a small round 1.5cm (⅝in) diameter piping tip. Pipe twelve 7cm (2¾in) long strips on the prepared baking tray. Bake for 20–22 minutes, rotating halfway through baking, or until the edges are golden brown but the centres are still pale. Turn off the oven and remove the cookies. To ensure the cookies are crisp all the way through, use a spatula to carefully lift the cookies onto a wire rack. Set the rack on the baking tray and place back in the oven and allow the cookies to rest, in the cooling oven, for 10 minutes. Remove the tray from the oven and allow the cookies to cool to room temperature.

For the filling, melt the chocolate using either a double boiler or a microwave and mix through the peppermint extract. Sandwich two cookies together with a little of the milk chocolate mixture. Pop in the refrigerator to set the chocolate.

If stored in a sealed container, these cookies will keep for 3–4 days.

Panela Brown Butter Shortbread

MAKES 6

Panela is an unrefined form of sugar where the cane juice is boiled and the liquid evaporates, leaving behind a solid form of sugar that is compressed into blocks and either sold as is or broken into a crystallized form like I use here. The flavour is molasses heavy with a hint of bitterness and a note of liquorice. While I love the flavour it gives the shortbread itself, I love the classic, sugar-dusted look of traditional shortbread, so I use white granulated sugar for dusting, but use more panela if you prefer.

115g (4oz/1 stick) unsalted butter, diced

50g (1¾oz/⅓ cup) panela sugar (see Note)

¼ teaspoon fine sea salt

½ teaspoon vanilla bean paste

150g (5½oz/1 cup + 3 tablespoons) plain (all-purpose) flour

Granulated sugar, for dusting (optional)

Line a 23 × 13cm (9 × 5in) loaf pan with a strip of parchment paper, so that the bottom of the pan is covered and the parchment overhangs the long sides of the pan, securing it in place with a couple metal binder clips.

To make the shortbread, we first need to brown the butter. Add the butter to a small saucepan and place over a medium heat. The butter will first bubble and splatter as the water content is cooked out, then once settled it will start to foam and at this point you want to watch carefully for the milk solids to turn the butter a nutty brown. Pour the browned butter into a mixing bowl and refrigerate until thick and spreadable.

Remove the butter from the refrigerator, pour in the sugar, then beat together for 3–5 minutes until pale and fluffy. Add the salt and vanilla and beat briefly to distribute. Add the flour and mix just until it forms a dough. Scrape the dough into your prepared loaf pan and press into an even layer. Refrigerate until firm.

Preheat the oven to 160°C (140°C Fan) 325°F, Gas Mark 3. Use a knife to score the shortbread into 6 fingers, then use a fork to dock each finger a few times. Bake for about 45 minutes, or until a pale golden colour. Remove the pan from the oven, turn off the heat and scatter over a little granulated sugar. Use the parchment paper to carefully lift the shortbread from the oven. Using your score lines as a guide, cut the shortbread into 6 individual fingers. Carefully separate the fingers and place on a baking tray, then pop the tray back into the oven, leaving the door slightly ajar, for 30 minutes. Remove from the oven and allow the shortbread to cool fully. Stored in a sealed container these will keep for up to a week.

NOTE Panela is commonly found in health food stores but more and more it can be found in traditional supermarkets and, of course, very easily online. Using any finely ground unrefined sugar such as jaggery, muscovado, maple or coconut will bring its own unique flavour. If you can't get your hands on any of these sugars, you can use this recipe, using regular white sugar, for a classic shortbread cookie.

Pistachio Egg Yolk Shortbread with Berry Glaze

MAKES 6

These vibrant cookies use a traditional method that seems to have fallen out of fashion but which makes for a particularly tender shortbread – the cookies are made with the yolks from hard-boiled eggs. The egg yolk helps to prevent excess gluten development and results in a lighter, more melt-in-the-mouth texture.

65g (2¼oz/¼ cup + 1 teaspoon) unsalted butter, at room temperature

40g (1½oz/3½ tablespoons) caster (superfine or granulated) sugar

Zest of ½ lemon

Pinch of fine sea salt

½ teaspoon vanilla bean paste

1 large egg, hard-boiled

100g (3½oz/¾ cup + 1 tablespoon) plain (all-purpose) flour

25g (1oz/scant ¼ cup) finely chopped pistachios

FOR THE BERRY GLAZE

25g (1oz) raspberries

60g (2¼oz/½ cup) icing (powdered) sugar, sifted

Pinch of fine sea salt

10g (¼oz/1 heaped tablespoon) roughly chopped pistachios

To make the shortbread, add the butter, sugar, lemon zest, salt and vanilla to a mixing bowl and, using an electric hand mixer, beat together until combined, about 2 minutes. Scoop the egg yolk from the egg, then add to the butter mixture and beat for a further 2–3 minutes until pale and fluffy, and no lumps of egg yolk remain. Add the flour and pistachios and mix on low speed just until a crumbly dough is formed.

Tip the mixture out onto the work surface and use your hands to bring it together as a uniform dough. Shape the dough into a log that has a diameter of about 6cm (2½in). Wrap the dough in clingfilm (plastic wrap) or a reusable alternative and refrigerate for at least 1 hour, or until firm.

Preheat the oven to 170°C (150°C Fan) 340°F, Gas Mark 3½ and line a baking tray (sheet pan) with parchment paper.

Using a sharp paring knife, slice the log of dough into 6 equal pieces and place on the prepared baking tray. Bake for 20–22 minutes, rotating halfway through baking, or until the edges of the shortbread are golden. To ensure the shortbread is fully baked, carefully flip one of the cookies over. If the base is evenly browned, the cookies are fully baked. If the centre looks a little dark, almost like it is a little damp, bake for a few minutes more. Remove and allow to cool before glazing.

To make the glaze, push the berries through a fine mesh sieve. You should end up with about 15g (½oz) worth of raspberry purée. Mix the purée together with the icing sugar and salt until you have a thick glaze. Dip the tops of the cookies into the glaze and sprinkle with the chopped pistachios. Set the cookies on the baking tray until the glaze sets.

If stored in a sealed container, these cookies will keep for 2–3 days.

Thin Mints (V)

MAKES 6

Throughout this book you may discover I have a little obsession with American supermarket cookies, call it imagined nostalgia. Growing up and existing on a diet of American sitcoms and movies, I heard the names of American cookies hundreds of times before I actually travelled there and finally tried them. I tried my first thin mint, a Girl Scout Cookie, in San Francisco. I found a troop of girl scouts selling them around the corner from my hotel. My stomach overwhelmed my brain and I bought 3 boxes (I was travelling solo!) and the thin mints were my favourite. These are my homage to those cookies.

50g (1¾oz/⅓ cup + 1 tablespoon) plain (all-purpose) flour

7g (¼oz/1 tablespoon) cocoa powder, preferably black cocoa

⅛ teaspoon bicarbonate of soda (baking soda)

⅛ teaspoon fine sea salt

40g (1½oz/2¾ tablespoons) unsalted vegan block butter, softened

50g (1¾oz/¼ cup) caster (superfine or granulated) sugar

⅛ teaspoon peppermint extract

FOR THE COATING

100g (3½oz) vegan dark chocolate

⅛ teaspoon peppermint extract

Cocoa nibs (optional)

Line a baking tray (sheet pan) with parchment paper.

In a small bowl, whisk together the flour, cocoa powder, bicarbonate of soda and salt (if the cocoa powder is lumpy, sifting this mixture is worth the added effort). In a separate bowl, use an electric hand mixer to beat together the vegan butter, sugar and peppermint extract until soft and creamy, about 2–3 minutes. Add the flour mixture and mix just until the flour disappears into the butter mixture, forming a crumbly dough. You know you can stop mixing when the mixture turns from a dusty grey colour to dark brown or black. Tip the dough out onto the work surface and use your hands to bring together as a uniform dough.

Divide the dough into 6 equal pieces and roll each one into a ball. Place them on the prepared baking tray, then use a flat-bottomed drinking glass to press into flat discs, about 5cm (2in) in diameter. The edges of the cookies will crack once flattened, so use a round cookie cutter to scoot back into a neat round shape. Refrigerate the cookies for 15 minutes before baking.

Preheat the oven to 160ºC (140ºC Fan) 325ºF, Gas Mark 3.

Bake for about 20 minutes. Remove and set aside until fully cooled.

To decorate, melt the chocolate using either a double boiler or a microwave and scrape into a small bowl, mixing through the peppermint extract. Dip each cookie into the chocolate, coating entirely. Use a fork to carefully lift the cookie from the chocolate, allowing the excess chocolate to drip back into the bowl. Place the cookie back on the baking tray and sprinkle with a few cocoa nibs if you like. Refrigerate until the chocolate has set.

If stored in a sealed container in the refrigerator, these cookies will keep for 4–5 days.

Tahini Jam Thumbprints

MAKES 6

When the bottom of the jar has the barest amount of tahini left, these are the cookies I make to ensure not a single drop goes to waste. Made with a dough similar to a shortbread, these little cookies are great for people who find most cookies too sweet and who love a sweet and salty combo. You can use any jam you like for the topping, but I love the pairing of tahini and raspberry; it is like the grown-up sibling of PB&J.

15g (½oz/1 tablespoon) unsalted butter, at room temperature

35g (1¼oz/2 tablespoons + 1 teaspoon) light brown sugar

½ teaspoon vanilla bean paste

35g (1¼oz/2 tablespoons) tahini

35g (1¼oz/¼ cup + ½ tablespoon) plain (all-purpose) flour

⅛ teaspoon baking powder

¼ teaspoon fine sea salt

1 tablespoon white sesame seeds

1 tablespoon black sesame seeds

1 large egg white, beaten

6 teaspoons raspberry jam

Line a small baking tray (sheet pan) with parchment paper.

To make the cookie dough, place the butter and sugar in a mixing bowl and beat together until light and creamy, about 2–3 minutes. Add the vanilla and tahini and mix for minute or so more until fully combined. Add the flour, baking powder and salt and mix together just until a dough is formed. Divide the dough into 6 equal pieces and roll each one into a ball. Place the balls on the prepared baking tray and use a teaspoon measure or your thumb to press a dip into each cookie. Refrigerate the cookies for 15 minutes.

Preheat the oven to 180ºC (160ºC Fan) 350ºF, Gas Mark 4. In a small bowl, mix together the two types of sesame seeds.

Remove the cookies from the refrigerator and brush all over with the beaten egg white. Dip into the sesame seeds so the entire cookie is coated. Place back on the baking tray and spoon a little jam onto the top of each cookie. Bake for about 16 minutes, rotating halfway through baking. The finished thumbprints will still look a little pale and will come out of the oven still soft and delicate, so allow to cool fully before moving. The finished cookies will be light, crisp on the outside and crumbly in the centre.

If stored in a sealed container, these cookies will keep for 3–4 days.

Double Chocolate Ginger Viennese Fingers

MAKES 6

When I was a kid, the Viennese finger was always one of the first things I would reach for when presented with a variety box of biscuits. These buttery and crisp cookies, dipped in a little chocolate, were heaven to me. Now as an adult this version has my heart. This buttery cookie is made with cocoa to make it extra chocolatey and the filling is no longer a simple buttercream: it is infused with ginger to make it a little more sophisticated than the original. But it's still coated in chocolate, of course.

95g (3¼oz/⅓ cup + 2 tablespoons) unsalted butter, very soft

¼ teaspoon vanilla extract

35g (1¼oz/5 tablespoons) icing (powdered) sugar

75g (2½oz/½ cup + 1½ tablespoons) plain (all-purpose) flour

15g (½oz/3 tablespoons) cocoa powder

1 tbsp cornflour (cornstarch)

Pinch of fine sea salt

FOR THE FILLING AND COATING

25g (1oz/2 tablespoons) unsalted butter, at room temperature

50g (1¾oz/¼ cup + 3 tablespoons) icing (powdered) sugar

Pinch of fine sea salt

10g (¼oz/1 heaped tablespoon) finely diced stem ginger, plus 1 tablespoon syrup from the jar

100g (3½oz) dark chocolate, melted

Line a baking tray (sheet pan) with parchment paper.

In a large bowl, beat together the butter, vanilla and icing sugar until soft and creamy, 2–3 minutes. It is very important that the butter starts at room temperature and the texture is very soft and creamy before you add the flour, otherwise the dough is hard to pipe. Sift in the flour, cocoa powder, cornflour and salt and mix with a spatula until an evenly combined dough is formed.

Scrape the dough into a piping bag fitted with a round star tip and pipe 7cm (2¾in) long strips onto the prepared baking tray. Chill the piped cookies for 20 minutes.

Preheat the oven to 180°C (160°C Fan) 350°F, Gas Mark 4.

Bake for about 12 minutes, or until they look dry. Remove the tray from the oven and set aside until fully cool.

For the filling, add the butter, icing sugar and salt to a bowl and beat together until light and fluffy, about 5 minutes. Add the stem ginger and the syrup and beat briefly until evenly distributed. Pipe or spread a layer of buttercream onto the bottom of half the cookies and sandwich together with a second cookie. To decorate, dip the cookies halfway into the melted chocolate, allowing any excess chocolate to drip back into the bowl. Set the chocolate-coated cookies back on the baking tray and refrigerate until the chocolate is set.

If stored covered, these cookies will keep for 2–3 days. They'll be fine for longer, but the buttercream will start to soften the cookies after that.

Bejewelled Biscotti

MAKES 6

These are the perfect cookie when the back of your cupboard is filled with the dregs of dried fruits and nuts, not enough to use for a bigger recipe but enough that they need a use. You can use just about any combination of dried fruits and nuts you have on hand and if you want to make these a little extra special, you can also drizzle them with or dunk them in some melted chocolate. If you like a hint of citrus, I also love throwing in a little candied peel.

85g (3oz/⅔ cup) plain (all-purpose) flour

½ teaspoon baking powder

⅛ teaspoon fine sea salt

35g (1¼oz/3 tablespoons) caster (superfine or granulated) sugar

50g (1¾oz/¼ cup + 2 tablespoons) mixed dried fruit

25g (1oz/3 tablespoons) raw, skin-on almonds

25g (1oz/¼ cup) roughly chopped pistachios

1 tablespoon honey

15g (½oz/1 tablespoon) unsalted butter, diced

1 large egg white

Preheat the oven to 180°C (160°C Fan) 350°F/Gas Mark 4 and line a baking tray (sheet pan) with parchment paper.

To make the biscotti dough, add the flour, baking powder, salt and sugar to a large bowl and whisk together. Add the fruit and nuts and stir to combine. Add the honey and butter to a small saucepan and place over a low heat until melted. Add the egg white and the melted butter mixture to the bowl and stir together until a rough dough is starting to form. To fully combine the ingredients, you'll need to get your hands in the bowl and gently knead together to form a uniform dough.

Form the dough into a 15cm (6in) long log and place on the prepared baking tray. Use your hands to press into a flat rectangle, roughly 12cm (4½in) wide. Bake for 25–30 minutes, or until a uniformly golden brown colour. Remove the tray from the oven and leave the biscotti to cool for 10 minutes.

Once cool enough to handle, use a large, serrated knife to cut into 6 equal biscotti. Turn cut-side down and bake for a further 10 minutes until crisp. Allow the biscotti to cool fully.

If the biscotti are properly dried out and kept in a sealed container, they will stray crisp for at least 2 weeks.

Knobbly Chocolate Oat Cookies

MAKES 4

One of the classic British biscuits, a knobbly chocolate oat cookie is an incredibly moreish treat. Toasty from brown sugar and oats, it's also crisp and a little bit crumbly. Sold in multiple varieties, I think it is fair to say that the chocolate-coated version reigns supreme and is therefore what I set out to replicate. It's rare that I would claim to make something better than the original, but these knock the commercial version out of the park. Incredibly easy to make, they are the ultimate treat to dunk in a big mug of tea.

35g (1¼oz/¼ cup + ½ tablespoon) wholemeal plain (all-purpose) flour

30g (1oz/2 tablespoons) light brown sugar

30g (1oz/⅓ cup) porridge oats (see Note)

¼ teaspoon bicarbonate of soda (baking soda)

¼ teaspoon fine sea salt

35g (1¼oz/2½ tablespoons) unsalted butter

½ tablespoon honey

50g (1¾oz) dark or milk chocolate, melted, for coating (optional)

To make the cookies, add the flour, sugar, oats, bicarbonate of soda and salt to a small bowl and mix together to combine. Melt the butter and honey together in a small saucepan set over a low heat, or using a microwave, then pour into the dry ingredients, mixing together to form a dough. The cookie dough will be a little crumbly but that is as it should be, so don't worry. Refrigerate the dough for 30 minutes before baking.

Preheat the oven to 180ºC (160ºC Fan) 350ºF, Gas Mark 4 and line a baking tray (sheet pan) with parchment paper.

Form the cookie dough into 4 equal pieces and roll each one into a ball. Place on the prepared baking tray and use a flat-bottomed drinking glass to press into rounds just over 7cm (2¾in) in diameter. Once pressed flat, the edges of the cookies will have cracked, so use a round cookie cutter to scoot back into neat, round 7cm (2¾in) circles. Bake for about 20 minutes, or until golden brown across the entire surface with the edges just a touch darker. Remove from the oven and allow to cool on the tray for 10 minutes before transferring to a wire rack to cool completely.

If coating them, spoon a little chocolate onto each of the cookies and spread to the edges, setting aside until the chocolate has set.

If stored in a sealed container, these cookies will keep for up to a week.

NOTE For these cookies you don't want to use jumbo rolled oats, you want something a little smaller, like regular porridge oats or even quick-cook oats. If all you have is jumbo or traditional rolled oats, break them down with a couple of pulses in a food processor.

Salted Malt Shortbread Rounds

MAKES 6

These delightfully simple shortbread-style cookies are a lesson in restraint and simple flavours. They start with a buttery shortbread-style dough and are gently flavoured with malt powder and finished with a little flaked sea salt to bring everything together and highlight the flavours of the cookie. To add a little texture, the outsides of the cookies are rolled in demerara sugar. Perfectly simple and perfectly delicious.

50g (1¾oz/3½ tablespoons) unsalted butter, diced and at room temperature

20g (¾oz/1 tablespoon + 2 teaspoons) caster (superfine or granulated) sugar

20g (¾oz/1 tablespoon + 1 teaspoon) light brown sugar

100g (3½oz/¾ cup + 1 tablespoon) plain (all-purpose) flour

2 tablespoons malted milk powder

Pinch of fine sea salt

FOR THE COATING

1 egg white, lightly beaten

Demerara (turbinado) sugar

Flaked sea salt

To make the dough, add the butter and sugars to a large bowl and beat with a spatula until pale and creamy, about 2 minutes. Add the flour, malt powder and salt and mix together just until a uniform dough is formed. Be careful to not overmix the dough as once the flour is added too much mixing can make for chewy, rather than crisp, cookies.

Turn the dough out onto a work surface and roll into a log roughly 5cm (2in) in diameter. Roll in clingfilm (plastic wrap) or a reusable alternative and refrigerate for at least 1 hour, or until firm.

Preheat the oven to 170°C (150°C Fan) 340°F, Gas Mark 3½ and line a baking tray (sheet pan) with parchment paper.

Remove the log of dough from the refrigerator and use a pastry brush to coat the outside in the egg white. Pour enough demerara sugar onto a small plate to cover, then roll the log of dough on the sugar, coating the entire outside. Using a sharp paring knife, carefully cut into 6 slices. Place the cookies on the prepared tray and sprinkle with a little flaked sea salt.

Bake for 17–18 minutes, or until golden around the edges. Remove and set aside until fully cool.

If stored in a sealed container, these cookies will keep for up to a week.

Vanilla Kipferl

MAKES 6

Many cultures around the world have some version of a nutty shortbread and, it is likely, they all share a similar origin, being traced back to the Middle East, spreading far and wide thanks to the spice routes. This particular version is from Austria, and its crescent shape and name is shared with the kipferl pastry, the precursor to modern croissants. Traditionally, these melt-in-the-mouth cookies are coated in icing sugar but I prefer to use a vanilla sugar. If you can get your hands on tonka beans, grating a little bit into your vanilla sugar makes these cookies otherworldly.

60g (2¼oz/¼ cup) unsalted butter, at room temperature

20g (¾oz/3 tablespoons) icing (powdered) sugar

½ teaspoon vanilla bean paste

75g (2½oz/½ cup + 1½ tablespoons) plain (all-purpose) flour

25g (1oz/¼ cup) finely ground pecans

Pinch of fine sea salt

50g (1¾oz/¼ cup) vanilla sugar (see Note), for coating

Add the butter and icing sugar to a mixing bowl and, using an electric hand mixer, beat for a couple minutes until smooth and creamy. Add the vanilla and beat to combine. Add the flour, nuts and salt and mix just until the flour is combined and a crumbly dough is formed.

Tip the mixture out onto a work surface and use your hands to bring together as a uniform dough. Refrigerate for 1 hour, or until the dough is firm.

Remove the dough from the refrigerator and cut into 6 equal pieces. Roll each piece of dough into 10–12cm (4–4½in) cylinder, with slightly tapered ends. Bend the cookies into a U shape and place on a parchment-lined baking tray (sheet pan). Refrigerate the cookies for 15 minutes.

Preheat the oven to 180°C (160°C Fan) 350°F, Gas Mark 4.

Bake for 15–17 minutes, or until a pale golden colour and firm to the touch. Remove from the oven and set aside for a couple minutes before completely coating in the vanilla sugar (the warmth of the cookies will help the sugar adhere).

If stored in a sealed container, these cookies will keep for up to a week.

NOTE You can buy vanilla sugar but it is also incredibly easy to make and a great way to use up spent vanilla pods. Once the seeds have been scraped out for another recipe, simply chop up the pods and add them to a jar of sugar, adding more as you use them. Leave the jar for a few weeks, shaking occasionally, until the sugar is fragrant.

OOEY GOOEY

Speculoos-Stuffed Dark Chocolate Cookies (V)

MAKES 2

How can something be this delicious but also so incredibly simple to make? The texture of these cookies is reminiscent of brownies but hiding inside is a surprise speculoos filling. As these are vegan and made with oil, the cookie dough is the work of mere seconds; basically, the payoff is significantly greater than the work would suggest.

15g (½oz/3 tablespoons) cocoa powder

25g (1oz/⅛ cup) caster (superfine or granulated) sugar

25g (1oz/2 tablespoons) light brown sugar

15ml (1 tablespoon) vegetable oil

15ml (1 tablespoon) soy milk (or other plant-based milk)

35g (1¼oz/¼ cup + ½ tablespoon) plain (all-purpose) flour

¼ teaspoon baking powder

Pinch of fine sea salt

Flaked sea salt (optional)

50g (1¾oz/3 heaped tablespoons) speculoos spread (I use Biscoff), for the filling

To a small mixing bowl, add the cocoa powder and sugars and whisk together to combine. Pour in the oil and milk and stir together until smooth and lump free. Add the flour, baking powder and salt and mix to form a uniform cookie dough. Pop in the refrigerator while you work on the filling.

Spoon the speculoos spread into 2 portions and set on a small plate, shaping each one into a rough ball. Pop the plate in the freezer for 30 minutes.

Preheat the oven to 180°C (160°C Fan) 350°F, Gas Mark 4 and line a small baking tray (sheet pan) with parchment paper.

Once the filling is chilled and firm, remove both the filling and cookie dough. Divide the dough in half and roll into balls. Flatten each ball of cookie dough into a disc and place the speculoos filling in the middle. Fold the cookie dough over the filling, pressing the edges together to seal, then roll into a neat round ball.

Place the cookies on the prepared baking tray and sprinkle with a little flaked sea salt if you wish. Bake for about 15 minutes, or until the cookies have spread and cracked around the edges. Remove and set aside to cool for 15 minutes.

If stored in a sealed container, these cookies will keep for 2–3 days.

Frosted Banana Bread Cookies

MAKES 6

Banana bread may be a perennial favourite but these banana bread cookies are much quicker to bake than a traditional loaf of bread, and ready in 30 minutes. These also have the delicious addition of a layer of cream cheese frosting, making these cake-like cookies a special and speedy treat. The key to a delicious banana cookie is the same as when making a loaf of banana bread – use bananas that are incredibly well ripened, soft and covered in dark spots.

60g (2¼oz/¼ cup) unsalted butter, softened

75g (2½oz/⅓ cup) light brown sugar

115g (4oz/½ cup) mashed banana

1 teaspoon vanilla extract

120g (4¼oz/1 cup) plain (all-purpose) flour

½ teaspoon bicarbonate of soda (baking soda)

¼ teaspoon fine sea salt

½ teaspoon ground cinnamon

⅛ teaspoon freshly grated nutmeg

FOR THE CREAM CHEESE FROSTING

50g (1¾oz/3½ tablespoons) unsalted butter, at room temperature

50g (1¾oz/scant ¼ cup) cream cheese, at room temperature

¼ teaspoon vanilla bean paste

Pinch of fine sea salt

75g (2½oz/½ cup + 2 tablespoons) icing (powdered) sugar

FOR DECORATION

6 banana chips

25g (1oz/scant ¼ cup) roughly chopped toasted pecans

NOTE These cookies can easily be made vegan with a couple of simple switches: swap the dairy butter for a vegan alternative and the cream cheese for a vegan option. Vegan cream cheese often lacks a real tang, so a few drops of lemon juice will help replicate the flavour.

Preheat the oven to 180°C (160°C Fan) 350°F, Gas Mark 4 and line a large baking tray (sheet pan) with parchment paper.

In a large bowl, mix together the butter, sugar, banana and vanilla, mixing until fully combined. Add the flour, bicarbonate of soda, salt, cinnamon and nutmeg and mix to form a cake-like batter. Using a 60ml (4 tablespoon/¼ cup) cookie scoop, portion the batter into rounds on the prepared baking tray, allowing plenty of space for the cookies to spread.

Bake for about 12 minutes, rotating halfway through baking, or until the edges are lightly browned and the centres are set. Remove and set aside to cool before adding the frosting.

To make the frosting, add the butter and cream cheese to a mixing bowl and beat together until soft, creamy and lump free. Add the vanilla and salt and mix together briefly to combine. Add the icing sugar in two batches, beating for a couple minutes until the frosting is light and fluffy. Divide the frosting between the cookies, spreading to cover most of the surface. To decorate, add a banana chip to each cookie and sprinkle with some roughly chopped pecans.

These cookies are best enjoyed within 2 days of baking.

Mexican Hot Chocolate Cookies

MAKES 4 LARGE COOKIES

These are GIANT cookies, like something you would get from a bakery. They would also be happy in a variety of chapters in this book; in Chewy or Chocolate Heaven as well as this Ooey Gooey chapter. The cookies are brownie-esque in flavour, with a hidden marshmallow in the centre giving them lots of chew. They are also lightly spiced so that they are reminiscent of Mexican hot chocolate. As the cookies bake, they will slightly erupt, revealing the molten marshmallow hidden within, also making them rather delicate when they come out of the oven; make sure to let them cool fully before trying to move them.

75g (2½oz/⅔ stick) unsalted butter, diced

100g (3½oz/scant ½ cup) light brown sugar

1 large egg yolk

½ teaspoon vanilla extract

75g (2½oz/½ cup + 1½ tablespoons) plain (all-purpose) flour

35g (1¼oz/⅓ cup + 2 tablespoons) cocoa powder

¼ teaspoon bicarbonate of soda (baking soda)

¼ teaspoon baking powder

¼ teaspoon chilli powder (see Note)

½ teaspoon ground cinnamon

¼ teaspoon fine sea salt

4 marshmallows

Demerara (turbinado) sugar, for coating

To make the cookies, melt the butter in either a small saucepan or in a heatproof bowl using a microwave. Pour the butter into a mixing bowl with the brown sugar and mix to combine. Add the egg yolk and vanilla and whisk until smooth and silky. Add the flour, cocoa powder, bicarbonate of soda, baking powder, spices and salt and mix to form a smooth cookie dough. Cover the bowl with clingfilm (plastic wrap) or a reusable alternative, and refrigerate for 15 minutes.

Preheat the oven to 180°C (160°C Fan) 350°F, Gas Mark 4 and line a baking tray (sheet pan) with parchment paper.

Remove the dough from the refrigerator and divide into 4 equal pieces. Roll each piece into a ball and then use your hands to flatten it into a large disc. Place a marshmallow onto the disc and fold the dough over to cover the marshmallow. Roll into a ball, sealing in the marshmallow. Then roll each cookie in demerara sugar and place on the prepared baking tray.

Bake for about 18–19 minutes, rotating halfway through baking, or until the cookies have spread and are cracked on top, revealing the marshmallow within. The edges of the cookies will be set but the centres will still be soft. Because of the marshmallow the cookies can expand and spread in an erratic manner. If you want the cookies to look neat and round, use a large round cookie cutter to scoot the cookies back into shape as soon as they come out of the oven. Set the cookies aside until fully cooled.

If stored in a sealed container, these cookies will keep for 3–4 days.

NOTE   Personally I like to use a chilli powder with a medium heat so that it doesn't overpower the chocolate, but feel free to use a spice level of your choice.

Tiramisu Cookies

MAKES 4

Tiramisu is, and will always be, my all-time favourite dessert – it's a perfect combination of flavours to make the most perfect of desserts. Transformed into a cookie, these are like a little hand-held version of the dessert. I haven't included any alcohol in the recipe but should you want that element, adding a splash of dark rum to the mascarpone cream will work wonders.

60g (2¼oz/¼ cup) unsalted butter, diced

2 teaspoons instant espresso powder

75g (2½oz/⅓ cup) light brown sugar

2 tablespoons whole milk

125g (4½oz/1 cup) plain (all-purpose) flour

½ teaspoon bicarbonate of soda (baking soda)

½ teaspoon fine sea salt

FOR THE MASCARPONE TOPPING

50g (1¾oz/3½ tablespoons) mascarpone

100ml (3½fl oz/⅓ cup + 1 tablespoon) double (heavy) cream

½ tablespoon light brown sugar

½ teaspoon vanilla bean paste

Cocoa powder, for dusting

For the cookies, melt the butter using either a small saucepan set over a medium heat or a microwave. Pour the melted butter into a mixing bowl and whisk in the instant coffee until dissolved. Add the sugar and milk and mix until smooth. Add the flour, bicarbonate of soda and salt and mix together until a smooth cookie dough is formed. Scrape the dough into a small bowl, cover with clingfilm (plastic wrap) or a reusable alternative and refrigerate for at least 1 hour, or until firm.

Preheat the oven to 180°C (160°C Fan) 350°F, Gas Mark 4 and line a baking tray (sheet pan) with parchment paper.

Divide the dough into 4 equal pieces and roll each one into a ball. Place on the prepared baking tray, setting them well apart to account for spreading. Bake for about 16 minutes, rotating halfway through baking, or until the edges are lightly browned. Remove and set aside for 5 minutes before transferring to a wire rack to cool completely.

For the topping, place the mascarpone, cream, sugar and vanilla in a large bowl and whisk together until the mixture holds soft peaks. Spoon the mascarpone cream on top of the cookies and spread to cover. Dust liberally with cocoa powder before serving.

These cookies will keep for 3–4 days without the topping, but once added they should be served on the same day, as the cream will slowly soften the cookies.

Triple Chocolate Skillet Cookie for Two

SERVES 2

We can all agree that there is little better than a fresh-from-the-oven chocolate chip cookie, when the centre is gooey and the chocolate still molten. If that statement rings true for you, then this is your perfect recipe. A dessert cookie for two, it is the ultimate treat for fans of ooey gooey cookies. The edges of the skillet cookie bake up nice and crisp but the majority of the cookie is soft and gooey, packed full of melted chocolate – a mixture of dark, milk and white – perfect served with a scoop of vanilla ice cream.

35g (1¼oz/2½ tablespoons) unsalted butter, diced, plus extra for greasing

30g (1oz/2 tablespoons) light brown sugar

30g (1oz/2½ tablespoons) caster (superfine or granulated) sugar

1½ tablespoons whole milk

70g (2½oz/½ cup + 1 tablespoon) plain (all-purpose) flour

¼ teaspoon baking powder

¼ teaspoon bicarbonate of soda (baking soda)

¼ teaspoon fine sea salt

50g (1¾oz) mix of milk, dark and white chocolate, roughly chopped

Flaked sea salt, for sprinkling

Preheat the oven to 180°C (160°C Fan) 350°F, Gas Mark 4. Lightly grease a small 15cm (6in) cast-iron skillet or a 15cm (6in) round cake tin.

Melt the butter in either a small saucepan set over a medium heat or using a microwave. Pour the butter into a small bowl along with the sugars and mix together until combined. Mix in the milk until the mixture is smooth. Add the flour, baking powder, bicarbonate of soda and salt and mix to form a soft cookie dough. Add the chocolate, reserving a little for the top, and mix until evenly distributed.

Scrape the cookie dough into the prepared skillet and press into an even layer. Scatter over the reserved chocolate and press into the cookie dough. Sprinkle the cookie with a little flaked sea salt. Bake for 18–20 minutes, or until the edges are golden but the centre is still pale. Remove and set aside for a few minutes before serving, topped with a scoop of vanilla ice cream.

NOTE If you want to make this vegan, you can easily switch out the dairy ingredients for vegan alternatives.

Black Forest Brownie Crinkles (GF)

MAKES 5 SANDWICH COOKIES

These are ridiculously fudgy cookies; a more accurate description would be barely set brownie batter. They are a reworked version of the brownie cookies I've been making for years, except these are flourless and mini, so perfect for a sandwich cookie. Using whipped cream and a cherry compote as the fillings, these are like hand-held Black Forest gateaux.

100g (3½oz) dark chocolate, 65–75% cocoa solids, finely chopped

50g (1¾oz/3½ tablespoons) unsalted butter, diced

1 large egg

50g (1¾oz/¼ cup) caster (superfine or granulated) sugar

50g (1¾oz/scant ¼ cup) light brown sugar

20g (¾oz/¼ cup) cocoa powder

1 tablespoon cornflour (cornstarch)

¼ teaspoon fine sea salt

Flaked sea salt, for sprinkling

FOR THE CHERRY COMPOTE AND FILLING

100g (3½oz) cherries, pitted and halved

1½ tablespoons caster (superfine or granulated) sugar

A couple of drops of almond extract (optional)

1½ tablespoons lemon juice

2 teaspoons cornflour (cornstarch)

120ml (4fl oz/½ cup) double (heavy) cream

¼ teaspoon vanilla extract

To make the cherry compote, place the cherries, sugar, almond extract (if using) and lemon juice in a small saucepan. Place the pan over a medium heat and cook for 2–3 minutes, or until the fruit has released a lot of juice and has started to soften, but not yet broken down. In a small bowl, whisk together the cornflour and 1 tablespoon of water to make a slurry. Pour this mixture into the saucepan and stir well to combine. Cook until the mixture is thick and syrupy, about 1–2 minutes more. Scrape the compote into a small bowl, cover with clingfilm (plastic wrap) or a reusable alternative and refrigerate until needed.

Preheat the oven to 180ºC (160ºC Fan) 350ºF, Gas Mark 4 and line a large baking tray (sheet pan) with parchment paper. Place the chocolate and butter into a bowl set over a pan of simmering water, stirring occasionally until fully melted. Remove and set aside for 5 minutes. Once the chocolate mixture is slightly cooled, add the egg and sugars to a large bowl and use an electric hand mixer to whisk for 2–3 minutes, or until pale and fluffy. Pour in the cooled chocolate mixture and stir to combine. Sift over the cocoa powder, cornflour and salt and stir together until you have a smooth brownie batter.

Using a 30ml (2 tablespoon) cookie scoop, portion the batter onto the baking tray, setting the cookies at least 5cm (2in) apart to allow for spreading. Sprinkle the top of the cookies with a little flaked salt and bake for 10 minutes. The cookies should come out of the oven domed with cracking on the surface; they will flatten slightly as they cool.

For the filling, whip the cream and vanilla just until starting to hold very soft peaks. Scrape into a piping bag fitted with a plain round tip. Onto the bottom of half the cookies, pipe a ring of cream around the edge and fill the centre with a spoonful of the cherry compote. Sandwich together with a second cookie.

Once assembled, these cookies are best kept refrigerated, and will keep for 2–3 days.

Chocolate-stuffed Churros Cookies

MAKES 2

When visiting Madrid, enjoying a plate of freshly fried churros and a mug of obscenely thick hot chocolate is almost mandatory. This recipe tries to transpose that moment of joy into an incredibly simple cookie. The vanilla cookie dough is stuffed with chocolate and, before baking, is rolled in cinnamon sugar. Enjoyed still warm from the oven, these cookies have a molten chocolate core and warm toasty notes from the cookie, taking me straight back to breakfast in Madrid.

40g (1½oz/2¾ tablespoons) unsalted butter, melted

40g (1½oz/3 tablespoons + 1 teaspoon) caster (superfine or granulated) sugar

1 large egg yolk

¼ teaspoon vanilla bean paste

70g (2½oz/½ cup + 1 tablespoon) plain (all-purpose) flour

¼ teaspoon baking powder

Pinch of fine sea salt

FOR THE FILLING

20g (¾oz) milk or dark chocolate, roughly chopped

FOR THE COATING

2 tablespoons granulated sugar

1 teaspoon ground cinnamon

To make the cookie dough, pour the butter and sugar into a small bowl and mix together. Add the egg yolk and vanilla and mix together until smooth. Add the flour, baking powder and salt and mix to form a dough. Refrigerate the cookie dough for 30 minutes.

Preheat the oven to 180°C (160°C Fan) 350°F, Gas Mark 4 and line a baking tray (sheet pan) with parchment paper.

Divide the cookie dough in half and roll into balls. Flatten the balls and place half of the chocolate onto each disc of cookie dough. Fold the sides of the cookie dough over the chocolate and roll back into a ball, sealing in the chocolate. In a small bowl, whisk together the sugar and cinnamon and roll each cookie in the spiced sugar. Place the cookies on the prepared baking tray.

Bake for 18–20 minutes, rotating halfway through baking, just until the edges of the cookies are very lightly browned. Remove from the oven and allow to cool for 5 minutes before enjoying.

Best served still warm from the oven.

Hazelnut Spread-stuffed Cookies

MAKES 6

These seemingly simple cookies are hiding a secret: they are stuffed to the brim full of glorious chocolate and hazelnut spread. Personally, I love the contrast of the simple vanilla cookie dough with the chocolate spread filling, but if you want to amp these up a level, you could add some roughly chopped chocolate to the cookie dough too.

100g (3½oz) chocolate hazelnut spread

60g (2¼oz/¼ cup) unsalted butter, diced

75g (2½oz/⅓ cup) light brown sugar

1 large egg yolk

1 tablespoon whole milk

½ teaspoon vanilla bean paste

125g (4½oz/1 cup) plain (all-purpose) flour

¼ teaspoon baking powder

¼ teaspoon bicarbonate of soda (baking soda)

¼ teaspoon fine sea salt

Flaked sea salt, for sprinkling

Before you make the cookie dough, prepare the filling. Scoop 6 tablespoons of the chocolate spread onto a plate lined with parchment paper. Pop the plate in the freezer for at least 1 hour before using.

For the cookie dough, melt the butter in either a saucepan set over a medium heat or in a heatproof bowl in a microwave. Add the sugar to a mixing bowl and pour over the melted butter, setting aside to cool slightly. Add the egg yolk, milk and vanilla and mix until a smooth, uniform batter is formed. Add the flour, baking powder, bicarbonate of soda and fine salt and mix until fully combined. Refrigerate the cookie dough for 30 minutes.

Preheat the oven to 180°C (160°C Fan) 350°F, Gas Mark 4 and line a baking tray (sheet pan) with parchment paper.

Divide the cookie dough into 6 equal pieces and roll each one into a ball. Flatten each ball of dough into a disc and place a frozen piece of chocolate spread in the middle, folding over the cookie dough to seal in the chocolate spread, rolling the dough back into a neat ball. Place the finished cookie dough balls on the prepared baking tray and sprinkle with a little flaked sea salt.

Bake for 14–15 minutes, rotating halfway through baking, until the cookies are golden around the edges but still a little pale in the centre. Remove from the oven and allow to cool on the tray for 10 minutes before carefully transferring to a wire rack to cool completely.

If stored in a sealed container, these cookies will keep for up to 4 days.

Pretzel Caramel Thumbprints

MAKES 6

If sweet and salty is your thing, these cookies are for you. Made with a light vanilla cookie dough, they are rolled in crushed salted pretzels and then filled with a dollop of salted caramel. Very simple to make and incredibly moreish, you may need to make a double batch.

60g (2¼oz/¼ cup) unsalted butter, at room temperature

50g (1¾oz/¼ cup) caster (granulated) sugar

¼ teaspoon vanilla extract

115g (4oz/⅔ + ¼ cup) plain (all-purpose) flour

Pinch of fine sea salt

FOR THE COATING AND FILLING

1 large egg white, lightly beaten

50g (1¾oz) salted pretzels, crushed into small pieces

60g (2¼oz/3 tablespoons) salted caramel (shop-bought or homemade)

In a large bowl, using an electric hand mixer or a wooden spoon, beat together the butter and sugar for 5 minutes, or until light and fluffy. Add the vanilla and beat briefly to combine. Add the flour and salt and mix just until a uniform dough is formed.

Divide the dough into 6 equal pieces and roll each one into a ball. Add the egg white to a small bowl and the pretzels to a small plate. Roll each ball of cookie dough in the egg white to lightly coat, then transfer to the pretzels and roll until completely coated. Place on the prepared baking tray and, using your thumb, press in the centre to make a well. Place the cookies in the refrigerator for 15–20 minutes.

Preheat the oven to 180°C (160°C Fan) 350°F, Gas Mark 4.

Bake for 17–18 minutes until the cookies are just starting to brown. Remove and set aside for 5 minutes before spooning in the caramel. Set aside until fully cooled and then sprinkle with a little flaked sea salt.

If stored in a sealed container, these cookies will keep for 2 days.

Toasted Coconut Alfajores

MAKES 6

My all-time favourite South American treat, these classic cookies are made from a tender and crumbly dough and sandwiched with lots of sweet and sticky dulce de leche. To satisfy my love of both the coconut- and chocolate-coated varieties, I have combined the two, coating the cookies in white chocolate and then toasted coconut flakes.

60g (2¼oz/½ cup) plain (all-purpose) flour

15g (½oz/2 tablespoons) cornflour (cornstarch)

⅛ teaspoon fine sea salt

50g (1¾oz/3½ tablespoons) unsalted butter, at room temperature

20g (¾oz/3 tablespoons) icing (powdered) sugar

1 large egg yolk

¼ teaspoon vanilla extract

FOR THE FILLING AND COATING

100g (3½oz/⅓ cup) dulce de leche

150g (5½oz) white chocolate, melted

50g (1¾oz/1 cup) toasted coconut flakes

To make the cookies, sift the flour, cornflour and salt into a large bowl and whisk to combine.

In a mixing bowl, combine the butter and icing sugar and beat together until soft and creamy, about 2–3 minutes. Add the egg yolk and vanilla and mix together until smooth and fully combined. Add the flour mixture and mix until a soft cookie dough is formed.

Divide the dough into 12 equal pieces and roll each one into a ball. Place the cookies on a large parchment-lined baking tray (sheet pan). Dust a flat-bottomed glass in flour and use to press each of the balls into a flat disc, roughly 5–6cm (2–2½in) in diameter. Pop the baking tray into the refrigerator for 20 minutes, or until the cookies are firm to the touch.

Preheat the oven to 180°C (160°C Fan) 350°F, Gas Mark 4.

Bake the chilled cookies for about 10 minutes, or until the edges of the cookies are just starting to brown. Remove from the oven and allow to cool for 5 minutes before transferring to a wire rack to cool completely. Spoon or pipe the dulce de leche onto the bottom of half of the cookies and sandwich together with a second cookie, gently pressing together so the dulce de leche pushes out to the edge of the cookies.

To coat, pour the melted chocolate into a small bowl. Drop the cookies, one at a time, into the chocolate using a fork, making sure all sides are fully coated. Lift from the chocolate, using the fork, allowing any excess chocolate to drip back into the bowl before setting back onto the parchment-lined baking tray. Before the chocolate has a chance to set, generously sprinkle the cookies with the toasted coconut, ensuring the tops and sides of the cookies are fully coated. Refrigerate until the chocolate is set.

If kept refrigerated, these cookies will keep for 3–4 days.

Lemon Curd Crinkles (GF)

MAKES 6

These cookies, inspired by classic amaretti, are bright and zingy, soft and tender, and, if you close your eyes, will transport you straight to Sorrento, as you enjoy some lemon granita or limoncello. The vibrant citrus flavour pairs beautifully with the almond to create an incredibly easy-to-make cookie.

85g (3oz/¼ cup + 3 tablespoons) caster (superfine or granulated) sugar

Zest of 1 lemon

125g (4½oz/1¼ cups) ground almonds (almond meal)

Pinch of fine sea salt

1 large egg white

Icing (powdered) sugar, for coating

100g (3½oz/5 tablespoons) lemon curd

To make the cookie dough, place the sugar and lemon zest in a large bowl and use your fingertips to rub the zest into the sugar, doing so until the sugar is damp and fragrant. Add the ground almonds and salt and mix to combine. In a separate bowl, whisk the egg white until light and frothy, then scrape into the almond mixture and mix with a spatula until evenly combined. Cover the dough with clingfilm (plastic wrap) or a reusable alternative and refrigerate for 1 hour.

Preheat the oven to 180ºC (160ºC Fan) 350ºF, Gas Mark 4 and line a baking tray (sheet pan) with parchment paper. Fill a small bowl with icing sugar.

Divide the cookie dough into 6 equal pieces and roll each one into a ball. Roll the balls in the bowl of icing sugar, gently compacting the sugar onto the cookies to create a generous coating. Place the cookies on the prepared baking tray and use a tablespoon measure to flatten them slightly, creating a depression in the middle of each one. Fill these depressions with the lemon curd.

Bake for 15–17 minutes, or until there is very small amount of colour on the cookies. Remove and set aside to cool.

If stored in a sealed container, these cookies will keep for up to 5 days.

SANDWICH COOKIES

Maple Creams

MAKES 6

You'd be forgiven for thinking that these maple creams were inspired by trips to Canada or Vermont but you'd be wrong. They are, in fact, inspired by Japan. In train stations across the country there are shops that sell omiyage, local souvenirs you buy for colleagues, friends or family back home. Usually, these gifts are edible and the choices seemingly endless. I am very fond of these simple maple cookies, which I bought in Tokyo station, and this is my attempt at a homemade version. I like to use maple sugar in the cookies to maximize the potential flavour but if you prefer you can use regular caster (superfine or granulated) sugar.

30g (1oz/3 tablespoons) maple sugar

50g (1¾oz/3½ tablespoons) unsalted butter, at room temperature

85g (3oz/⅔ cup) plain (all-purpose) flour, plus extra for dusting

⅛ teaspoon fine sea salt

FOR THE FILLING

25g (1oz/1¾ tablespoons) unsalted butter, at room temperature

1½ tablespoons maple syrup

75g (2½oz/scant ⅔ cup) icing (powdered) sugar

Large pinch of flaked sea salt

To make the cookie dough, add the sugar and butter to a large bowl and, using an electric hand mixer or wooden spoon, cream together for 2–3 minutes, or until light and creamy. Add the flour and salt and mix until a uniform dough is formed. Tip the dough onto your work surface and shape into a rough square. Wrap in clingfilm (plastic wrap) or a reusable alternative and refrigerate for 1 hour.

Preheat the oven to 160ºC (140ºC Fan) 325ºF, Gas Mark 3 and line a baking tray (sheet pan) with parchment paper.

On a lightly floured work surface, roll the dough into a 13.5 × 18cm (5¼ × 7in) rectangle. Cut the dough into three 18cm (7in) long strips and then cut each strip into 4 squares. Place the cookies on the prepared baking tray. If the cookies have warmed up and are soft, refrigerate for 15 minutes before baking.

Bake for 16–18 minutes, or until the edges of the cookies are starting to brown. Remove and set aside to cool.

For the filling, add the butter to a large bowl and, using an electric hand mixer, beat until very soft and creamy. Add the maple syrup and beat until evenly combined. Add the icing sugar and salt and beat on low speed until combined, then beat on high speed for about 5 minutes, or until light and fluffy.

Spoon or pipe the filling onto the base of half the cookies and sandwich together with a second cookie.

If stored in a sealed container, these cookies will keep for 2–3 days.

Oatmeal Cream Pies

MAKES 4

When it comes to cookies, chocolate chip may be my ride or die, but a soft oatmeal cookie comes a very close second. Oatmeal cookies, with or without raisins, may also be the ultimate form of nostalgic baking; they taste almost old-fashioned, classic in their flavour, and confident in their unwavering form. Shop-bought oatmeal cream pies use a marshmallow-based filling, but I love the rich creaminess that comes with using a cream cheese frosting instead, which also happens to be less fussy and easier to make.

125g (4½oz/½ cup + 1 tablespoon) unsalted butter, at room temperature

150g (5½oz/⅔ cup) light brown sugar

3 tablespoons golden syrup (or honey)

1 tablespoon whole milk

200g (7oz/1½ cups + 1 tablespoon) plain (all-purpose) flour

1 teaspoon ground cinnamon

½ teaspoon fine sea salt

1 teaspoon bicarbonate of soda (baking soda)

150g (5½oz/1¾ cups + 2 tablespoons) traditional rolled oats

FOR THE CREAM CHEESE FILLING

50g (1¾oz/3½ tablespoons) unsalted butter, at room temperature

100g (3½oz/heaped ¾ cup) icing (powdered) sugar

50g (1¾oz/scant ¼ cup) cream cheese, at room temperature

¼ teaspoon vanilla bean paste

Pinch of fine sea salt

To make the cookie dough, in a small saucepan, combine the butter, sugar, golden syrup and milk and cook over a low–medium heat until fully melted, not allowing the mixture to bubble. Pour the mixture into a small bowl and set aside until cooled to room temperature. Add the remaining ingredients and mix to form a soft dough. Cover with clingfilm (plastic wrap) or a reusable alternative and refrigerate for 30 minutes before baking.

Preheat the oven to 180ºC (160ºC Fan) 350ºF, Gas Mark 4 and line a large baking tray (sheet pan) with parchment paper.

Divide the dough into 8 equal pieces, then roll each one into a ball. Place on the prepared baking tray, leaving plenty of space between each cookie. Bake for about 10 minutes, or until lightly browned around the edges and the centres are set but still a little pale. Allow the cookies to cool fully on the baking tray.

For the filling, beat together the butter and icing sugar until light and fluffy, about 5 minutes. Add the cream cheese, vanilla and salt and beat together just enough to make a smooth, lump-free buttercream.

To assemble, place a large dollop of the filling on half of the cookies and sandwich together with a second cookie.

Once assembled, the cookies will keep for 2–3 days in a sealed container but will get softer the older they get.

NOTE These cookies are easy to veganize should you wish – simply replace the butter and cream cheese with vegan alternatives. They also work very well with a gluten-free plain (all-purpose) flour.

Salted Caramel Sablé Breton

MAKES 6

If there is a place I belong, spiritually, it must surely be Brittany, in France. Home to the best butter, the most beautiful salts and salted butter caramel, I would surely be incredibly happy among my favourite things. These French sablés, a classic cookie from the Breton region, celebrate all of these ingredients. The cookies are rich in butter and use salt to highlight all the flavour that the butter brings to the table. To sandwich the cookies, a combination of vanilla buttercream and salted caramel is used to make these rustic cookies into something a little bit more elaborate.

2 large egg yolks

30g (1oz/¼ cup) icing (powdered) sugar

35g (1¼oz/2½ tablespoons) unsalted butter, softened

60g (2¼oz/scant ½ cup) plain (all-purpose) flour, plus extra for dusting

¼ teaspoon fine sea salt

¼ teaspoon baking powder

FOR THE SALTED CARAMEL

50g (1¾oz/¼ cup) caster (superfine or granulated) sugar

Pinch of flaked sea salt

30ml (2 tablespoons) double (heavy) cream

5g (1 teaspoon) unsalted butter

FOR THE VANILLA BUTTERCREAM

25g (1oz/2 tablespoons) unsalted butter, at room temperature

50g (1¾oz/¼ cup + 3 tablespoons) icing (powdered) sugar

Pinch of fine sea salt

¼ teaspoon vanilla bean paste

To make the sablés, add 1 egg yolk and the icing sugar to a mixing bowl and, using an electric hand mixer, whisk together for a minute or so. Add the butter and mix until smooth and fully combined. Add the flour, salt and baking powder and mix until a soft dough forms. Wrap the dough in clingfilm (plastic wrap) or a reusable alternative and press it into a flat disc. Refrigerate for at least 1 hour, or until firm.

Meanwhile, for the salted caramel, add the sugar to a small saucepan and place over a medium heat. Once melted and caramelized, resembling the colour of an old penny, remove the pan from the heat and add the salt, cream and butter, stirring to form a smooth caramel. If lumps form, place the pan over a low heat and stir until smooth. Scrape the caramel into a small bowl and set aside to cool.

On a lightly floured work surface, roll out the chilled dough until 5mm (¼in) thick. Using a 5cm (2in) round cookie cutter, cut out as many rounds of dough as possible. Re-roll the scraps and cut out more rounds of dough. Place the cookies on a parchment-lined baking tray (sheet pan) and refrigerate the cookies for 20 minutes.

Preheat the oven to 180ºC (160ºC Fan) 350ºF, Gas Mark 4. Beat the remaining egg yolk and use it to brush the cookies. Then use a fork to score a cross-hatch pattern on the top of each cookie. Bake for about 18 minutes, or until golden brown. Remove and set aside until fully cooled.

For the buttercream, beat together the butter and icing sugar until light and fluffy, about 5 minutes. Add the salt and vanilla and beat for 30 seconds to incorporate. Using a piping bag, pipe a ring of buttercream onto the base of half of the cookies and fill the centre of each ring with a little caramel. Sandwich together with a second cookie.

Once assembled, the cookies are good for up to 2 days stored in a sealed container.

Blackberry and Anise Linzers

MAKES 6

Linzer cookies are simple sandwich cookies, made with a nut-based dough and filled with jam, inspired by the famous Austrian torte of the same name. This version is all about the combination of star anise and blackberry, an absolute smash hit of a pairing.

80g (2¾oz/⅔ cup) plain (all-purpose) flour

20g (¾oz/3 tablespoons) ground almonds (almond meal)

⅛ teaspoon fine sea salt

55g (2oz/3½ tablespoons) unsalted butter, at room temperature

50g (1¾oz/¼ cup) caster (superfine or granulated) sugar

Seeds from 1 star anise, finely ground

1 tablespoon whole milk

¼ teaspoon vanilla bean paste

6 teaspoons blackberry jam, for the filling

To make the linzer dough, add the flour, ground almonds and salt to a bowl and mix to combine. In a separate bowl, using an electric hand mixer, beat together the butter, sugar and ground star anise for 2–3 minutes, or until light and creamy. Add the milk and vanilla bean paste and mix briefly to combine. Add the flour mixture and mix just until a uniform dough is formed.

Tip the dough out onto a work surface and use your hands to bring it together. Press into a flat disc, wrap in clingfilm (plastic wrap) or a reusable alternative and refrigerate for 1 hour, or until firm.

On a lightly floured worksurface, roll out the dough until it is roughly 4mm (¼in) thick and, using a 6cm (2½in) round cookie cutter, cut out as many discs as possible. Place the cookies on a parchment-lined baking tray (sheet pan) and use a small round cookie cutter to cut out the centre of half the cookies. Gather up the scraps and gently knead back into a uniform dough. Refrigerate the dough for 10 minutes before re-rolling and cutting out more cookies, as before. You should have 12 cookies in total – 6 tops and 6 bottoms, enough to make 6 sandwich cookies. Chill the cookies in the refrigerator for 10 minutes before baking.

Preheat the oven to 160°C (140°C Fan) 325°F, Gas Mark 3.

Bake for 20 minutes, or until the edges are just starting to brown. Remove the tray from the oven and set aside until cooled.

Spoon a little of the blackberry jam onto each of the bottom cookies, spreading it almost to the edge. Dust the top cookies with icing sugar and sandwich together with the bottom cookies.

Once filled with jam, the cookies will keep for 2 days, but without the filling the cookies will stay crisp for 3–4 days.

NOTE These cookies are particularly easy to veganize – simply swap the milk and butter for vegan alternatives.

Black Cocoa and Vanilla Sandwich Cookies

MAKES 6

Simple but nostalgic, these cookies get their characteristic flavour from their use of black cocoa, which is worth tracking down for this recipe alone (although it's a staple in my baking and is a favourite ingredient for dramatic bakes). Whatever you do, make sure you serve these with a glass of milk to really hone in on the nostalgia.

65g (2¼oz/½ cup) plain (all-purpose) flour

10g (¼oz/2 tablespoons) black cocoa powder

⅛ teaspoon bicarbonate of soda (baking soda)

⅛ teaspoon fine sea salt

50g (1¾oz/3½ tablespoons) unsalted butter

30g (1oz/2½ tablespoons) caster (superfine or granulated) sugar

30g (1oz/2 tablespoons) light brown sugar

FOR THE VANILLA BUTTERCREAM FILLING

15g (½oz/1 tablespoon) unsalted butter, softened

30g (1oz/¼ cup) icing (powdered) sugar

¼ teaspoon vanilla bean paste

Pinch of fine sea salt

½ tablespoon double (heavy) cream

To make the cookie dough, mix together the flour, cocoa powder, bicarbonate of soda and salt. In a separate bowl, using an electric hand mixer, beat together the butter and sugars, for 2–3 minutes or until pale and creamy. Add the flour mixture and mix together on low speed, just until the flour disappears into the butter mixture. The mixture will still be crumbly but it will change from a greyish colour to a darker black mixture and will hold together when squeezed. If you overmix this dough, the finished cookies can end up chewy and not crisp.

Tip the crumbly dough out onto the work surface and use your hands to bring it together into a uniform dough. Form into a rough log shape and transfer to a large sheet of clingfilm (plastic wrap) or a reusable alternative. Roll and shape the log so that it is roughly 5cm (2in) thick. Roll up in the clingfilm and refrigerate for at least 1 hour, or until firm.

Line 2 baking trays (cookie sheets) with parchment paper. Using a sharp paring knife, slice the log into 12 cookies (I measure the length of the log and divide it by 12 so each cookie is the same thickness). Place the cookies on the prepared baking tray and, if they've softened, pop the tray back into refrigerator for 15 minutes to firm up.

Preheat the oven to 180ºC (160ºC Fan) 350ºF, Gas Mark 4.

Bake for 11–12 minutes. As the cookies are made with cocoa it is hard to tell when they are done using visual cues, but they will be set around the outside and a little soft in the centre.

For the buttercream, add the butter to a bowl and, using an electric hand mixer, beat until soft and creamy. Add the icing sugar, vanilla and salt and beat for about 5 minutes, or until light and fluffy. Add the cream and mix until fully combined. Spoon or pipe the filling onto the base of half of the cookies and sandwich together with a second.

If stored in a sealed container, these cookies will keep for 2–3 days.

Ginger and Lemon Ice Cream Sandwiches

MAKES 6

I am an ice cream for all seasons type of person, not one of those odd people who tell you ice cream is only for the summer. Joy should not be limited to one season! These ice cream sandwiches are perfect year round, but my favourite time to enjoy them is in winter, when it's beautiful and sunny but also freezing cold. The warmth of ginger provides cosiness and the lemon gives a zingy complementary flavour.

100g (3½oz/¼ cup + 3 tablespoons) unsalted butter, diced

75g (2½oz/3½ tablespoons) golden syrup (or honey)

125g (4½oz/½ cup + 1 tablespoon) light brown sugar

1 large egg

220g (7¾oz/1¾ cups) plain (all-purpose) flour

¾ teaspoon bicarbonate of soda (baking soda)

¾ teaspoon fine sea salt

2 tablespoons ground ginger

1½ teaspoons ground cinnamon

Demerara (turbinado) sugar, for coating

FOR THE LEMON NO-CHURN ICE CREAM

600ml (20fl oz/2½ cups) double (heavy) cream

200ml (7fl oz/¾ cup + 1 tablespoon) condensed milk

½ teaspoon vanilla bean paste

200g (7oz/scant ⅔ cup) lemon curd

Line a 33 × 23cm/13 × 9in rimmed baking tray (sheet pan) with clingfilm (plastic wrap) or parchment paper.

To make the no-churn ice cream, add the cream, condensed milk and vanilla to a large bowl and whisk just until the mixture holds soft peaks. Scrape the mixture into the prepared sheet tray and spread into an even layer. Dollop over the lemon curd and gently swirl into the ice cream. Cover the surface of the ice cream with clingfilm and freeze for at least 4 hours.

To make the cookies, add the butter, golden syrup and brown sugar to a small saucepan and heat over a medium heat until the butter is melted. Pour into a mixing bowl and set aside to cool slightly. Whisk in the egg before adding the flour, bicarbonate of soda, salt and spices and then mixing together to form a soft, almost batter-like, dough. Cover with clingfilm or a reusable alternative and refrigerate for 1 hour, or until firm but pliable.

Preheat the oven to 180ºC (160ºC Fan) 350ºF, Gas Mark 4 and line 2 large baking trays (cookie sheets) with parchment paper.

Divide the dough into 12 equal pieces and roll each one into a ball. Roll the balls in demerara sugar, then place 6 cookies on each baking tray. Bake for about 12 minutes until spread and the edges are lightly browned. Remove and set aside to cool.

Remove the ice cream from the freezer and, using a cookie cutter roughly the same size as the cookies, cut out 6 pucks of ice cream and sandwich between 2 cookies. If not serving immediately, freeze the cookies for up to 2 weeks.

Without the ice cream, the cookies will keep for 4–5 days in a sealed container.

Toasted Flour Shortbread with Raspberry Filling

MAKES 6

These incredibly simple shortbread-style cookies get a flavour boost from using toasted flour, which adds a warm nuttiness. Paired simply with a raspberry buttercream, they are surprisingly complex and show what you can do with just the simplest of ingredients. If going to the lengths of toasting the flour, it is worth making more than you need so you are ready to go next time you make this recipe, or for making the Toasty Malty Milk Chocolate Chunk Cookies (page 145).

90g (3¼oz/scant ¾ cup) plain (all-purpose) flour

60g (2¼oz/¼ cup) unsalted butter, at room temperature

45g (1½oz/heaped ⅓ cup) icing (powdered) sugar

1 large egg yolk

¼ teaspoon vanilla bean paste

¼ teaspoon fine sea salt

FOR THE RASPBERRY BUTTERCREAM

25g (1oz/2 tablespoons) unsalted butter, at room temperature

40g (1½oz/⅓ cup) icing (powdered) sugar

25g (1oz/1 heaped tablespoon) raspberry jam

Pinch of fine sea salt

Before making the dough, we need to toast the flour. Add the flour to a saucepan, place over a medium heat and cook, stirring regularly with a spatula, for about 10 minutes or until the flour turns a golden colour, similar to malt powder, and smells almost like freshly popped popcorn. Scrape onto a plate or small baking tray (sheet pan) and set aside to cool. Once cooled, sift to remove any clumps. Store in a sealed container until needed.

To make the shortbread dough, add the butter and icing sugar to a mixing bowl and beat together until light and creamy, about 2–3 minutes. Add the egg yolk and vanilla and mix briefly just until combined. Add the flour and salt and mix until a soft, uniform dough forms. Scrape the dough onto a lightly floured work surface and shape it into a log, about 5cm (2in) in diameter. Wrap in clingfilm (plastic wrap) and refrigerate for 2–3 hours until firm.

Preheat the oven to 180ºC (160ºC Fan) 350ºF, Gas Mark 4 and line a baking tray (sheet pan) with parchment paper.

When the dough is solid, remove from the refrigerator and use a very sharp knife to cut the log into 12 equal rounds of dough. Place on the prepared baking tray, leaving a little space between each cookie. Bake for 12–14 minutes, or until golden. Remove from the oven and allow the cookies to cool for 5 minutes before transferring to a wire rack to cool completely.

For the raspberry buttercream, add the butter to a mixing bowl and beat until pale and creamy. Add the icing sugar in two batches, beating until combined before adding more. Once all the icing sugar has been added, beat for a further minute or so until light and fluffy. Add the jam and salt and beat together until fully combined.

Add a dollop of the filling onto the base of half of the cookies and sandwich together with a second cookie.

Once baked, the cookies will keep for 3–4 days but once assembled they are best enjoyed within 1–2 days, as the buttercream will slowly soften the cookies as they sit.

Sticky Toffee Sandwich Cookies

MAKES 5

It's safe to say that sticky toffee pudding ranks very highly among people's favourite desserts, especially here in the UK. These cookies are the sibling of the dessert, but instead of a date cake they're made with date cookies. Rather than a hot butterscotch sauce, the filling is chilled and then whipped and used to turn these into delicious, dessert-inspired sandwich cookies.

75g (2½oz/heaped ½ cup) roughly chopped dried dates

60g (2¼oz/¼ cup) unsalted butter, at room temperature

70g (2½oz/⅓ cup) light brown sugar

1 tablespoon whole milk

¼ teaspoon vanilla extract

120g (4¼oz/scant 1 cup) plain (all-purpose) flour

1 teaspoon ground cinnamon

1 teaspoon ground ginger

¼ teaspoon bicarbonate soda (baking soda)

¼ teaspoon fine sea salt

FOR THE WHIPPED BUTTERSCOTCH FILLING

50g (1¾oz/¼ cup) light brown sugar

40g (1½oz/2¾ tablespoons) unsalted butter, diced

25ml (1½ tablespoons) double (heavy) cream

large pinch of flaked sea salt

To make the butterscotch filling, add all the ingredients to a small saucepan and cook over a medium heat until everything is melted. Once melted and smooth, bring to a simmer and cook for 2 minutes. Pour into a small bowl and set aside for 5 minutes, then cover with clingfilm (plastic wrap) or a reusable alternative and refrigerate for 2 hours. To whip, the texture needs to be firm but scoopable.

To make the cookies, add the dates to a small bowl and pour over 25ml (1f oz) boiling water, then set aside for 10 minutes.

Add the butter and sugar to a large bowl and, using an electric hand mixer, beat together for about 5 minutes, or until light and fluffy. Add the milk and vanilla and mix briefly to combine. In a separate bowl, mix together the flour, spices, bicarbonate of soda and salt. Add the dry ingredients to the butter mixture and mix to form a dough. Drain off any excess water from the dates, then mix them through the cookie dough. Cover with clingfilm (plastic wrap) or a reusable alternative and refrigerate for 1 hour.

Preheat the oven to 160ºC (140ºC Fan) 325ºF, Gas Mark 3 and line 2 baking trays (cookie sheets) with parchment paper.

Using a 30ml (2 tablespoon) cookie scoop, divide the dough into 12 equal pieces and deposit the cookies onto the prepared baking trays, setting them well apart to account for spreading. Flatten each one slightly with your hands. Bake for about 18 minutes, or until the edges of the cookies are golden. Remove from the oven and set aside to cool.

Remove the butterscotch filling from the refrigerator and scrape into a large bowl. Using an electric hand mixer, whisk until light and fluffy, about 2 minutes.

To assemble, spoon or pipe the whipped butterscotch onto the base of half of the cookies and sandwich with a second cookie.

If stored in a sealed container, these cookies will keep for up to 2 days.

Chocolate and Peanut Butter Sandwich Cookies (GF)

MAKES 4

This sandwich cookie is a take on the classic peanut butter cookie, the old-fashioned, but still delicious, type that is flattened with a fork and bears the familiar crosshatch pattern. For this version, the cookies are made with oat flour, which gives them more flavour and adds a delicious chewy texture. The cookies are also sandwiched with both peanut butter frosting and a small amount of chocolate ganache.

30g (1oz/2 tablespoons) unsalted butter, at room temperature

75g (2½oz/⅓ cup) light brown sugar

1 tablespoon whole milk

½ teaspoon vanilla extract

75g (2½oz/¼ cup + ½ tablespoon) smooth peanut butter

75g (2½oz/heaped ¾ cup) oat flour

35g (1¼oz/¼ cup + 3 tablespoons) traditional rolled oats

⅛ teaspoon baking powder

¼ teaspoon bicarbonate of soda (baking soda)

¼ teaspoon fine sea salt

FOR THE CHOCOLATE GANACHE

35ml (2 tablespoons + 1 teaspoon) double (heavy) cream

35g (1¼oz) milk chocolate, finely chopped

FOR THE PEANUT BUTTER FROSTING

25g (1oz/2 tablespoons) unsalted butter, very soft

25g (1oz/1¾ tablespoons) smooth peanut butter

50g (1¾oz/¼ cup + 3 tablespoons) icing (powdered) sugar

Pinch of fine sea salt

Preheat the oven to 180ºC (160ºC Fan) 350ºF, Gas Mark 4 and line a baking tray (sheet pan) with parchment paper.

To make the cookies, place the butter and sugar in a large bowl and, using an electric hand mixer, beat together for 2–3 minutes until pale and creamy. Add the milk, vanilla and peanut butter and beat for a further 2 minutes, or until fully combined and smooth. In a separate bowl, whisk together the flour, oats, baking powder, bicarbonate of soda and salt. Add the flour mixture to the peanut butter mixture and mix until a uniform dough is formed. Divide into 10 equal pieces and roll each one into a ball. Place on the prepared baking tray and use a flat-bottomed glass to flatten each one into a 6cm (2½in) diameter disc.

Bake for 15–17 minutes, or until the edges are starting to brown. Remove and set aside to cool.

While the cookies are baking, make the ganache. Add the cream and chocolate to a small bowl and heat together in a microwave until the chocolate has melted, then mix together to form a smooth ganache. Set aside until needed.

To make the frosting, add the butter and peanut butter to a bowl and beat together until soft and creamy, about 2–3 minutes. Add the icing sugar and salt and beat together for a couple minutes, or until light and fluffy.

To assemble, pipe or spread the frosting onto the base of half of the cookies, spreading so most of the cookie is covered. Spoon some ganache on top of the buttercream and spread to cover. Sandwich together with a second cookie.

If stored in a sealed container, these cookies will keep for 2–3 days but will soften as they sit.

NOTE When baking it is best to use a commercial peanut butter, as natural peanut butters can separate and cause issues with texture and spreading.

Lemon Custard Creams

MAKES 6

Out of all the British supermarket cookies, the custard cream may be my favourite. It's so simple but it's also texture and flavour perfection. A crisp cookie sandwiched with a creamy custard-flavoured filling. My version includes a gentle hint of lemon to add a little brightness, and I also increased the size because one of the shop-bought version is never quite enough.

110g (3¾oz/¾ cup + 2 tablespoons) plain (all-purpose) flour, plus extra for dusting

25g (1oz/3 tablespoons) custard powder

⅛ teaspoon fine sea salt

85g (3oz/¼ cup + 2 tablespoons) unsalted butter, at room temperature

40g (1½oz/3½ tablespoons) caster (superfine or granulated sugar)

¼ teaspoon vanilla extract

FOR THE LEMON FILLING

40g (1½oz/3 tablespoons) unsalted butter, at room temperature

80g (2¾oz/⅔ cup) icing (powdered) sugar

Zest of 1 lemon

Pinch of fine sea salt

2 teaspoons lemon juice

To make the cookie dough, place the flour, custard powder and salt in a bowl and whisk together to combine. In a separate bowl, combine the butter and sugar and, using an electric hand mixer, beat together until light and creamy, about 2–3 minutes. Add the flour mixture and mix together to form a crumbly dough. Tip the mixture out onto a work surface and use your hands to bring together into a uniform dough. Shape into a rough rectangle shape, wrap in clingfilm (plastic wrap) or a reusable alternative, then refrigerate for at least 1 hour before rolling out.

Preheat the oven to 160°C (140°C Fan) 325°F, Gas Mark 4 and line a baking tray (sheet pan) with parchment paper.

On a lightly floured work surface, roll out the dough into a 24 × 15cm (9½ × 6in) rectangle. Cut into three 24cm (9½in) long strips, then cut each strip into 4 rectangular cookies. Place the cookies on the prepared baking tray, then dock each cookie a few times with a fork.

Bake for about 20 minutes, or until the edges are golden brown. Remove and set aside to cool.

For the filling, add the butter to a large bowl and, using an electric hand mixer, beat until pale and creamy. Add the icing sugar, lemon zest and salt and beat together for about 5 minutes or until light and fluffy. Add the lemon juice and mix briefly to combine. Pipe or spread the filling onto the base of half of the cookies and sandwich together with a second cookie.

If stored in a sealed container, these cookies will keep for 2–3 days.

NOTE If you can't find custard powder, a typical British ingredient, you can switch it one for one for cornflour (cornstarch).

Red Velvet Sandwich Cookies

MAKES 6

Red velvet was probably last cool in the early 2000s but maybe I'm just not cool, because it is still one of my favourite cakes. A mild cocoa sponge, sandwiched with cream cheese frosting, what's not to love?! These soft and spongy cookies are similarly sandwiched with cream cheese frosting, and if you don't think these are the cutest thing ever, I'm sorry but we can't be friends.

70g (2½oz/¼ cup + 1 tablespoon) unsalted butter, at room temperature

40g (1½oz/3½ tablespoons) caster (superfine or granulated) sugar

40g (1½oz/3 tablespoons) light brown sugar

1 large egg

2 teaspoons red gel paste food colouring

100g (3½oz/¾ cup + 1 tablespoon) plain (all-purpose) flour

25g (1oz/¼ cup + 1 tablespoon) cocoa powder

½ teaspoon bicarbonate soda (baking soda)

¼ teaspoon fine sea salt

FOR THE CREAM CHEESE FILLING

40g (1½oz/2¾ tablespoons) unsalted butter, diced and at room temperature

80g (2¾oz/⅔ cup) icing (powdered) sugar

¼ teaspoon vanilla bean paste

Pinch of fine sea salt

40g (1½oz/3 tablespoons) cream cheese

Preheat the oven to 180°C (160°C Fan) 350°F, Gas Mark 4 and line a couple baking trays (cookie sheets) with parchment paper.

Add the butter and sugars to a large bowl and use an electric hand mixer to beat until light and fluffy, about 5 minutes. Add the egg and food colouring and beat together until fully combined. Add the flour, cocoa powder, bicarbonate of soda and salt and mix together until a soft cookie dough is formed.

Using a 30ml (2 tablespoon) cookie scoop, portion out the cookie dough onto the prepared baking trays. Bake for about 10 minutes, or until the cookies are set and feel springy in the centre. Remove the baking trays from the oven and set aside for 10 minutes before transferring the cookies to a wire rack to cool completely.

For the filling, add the butter to a bowl and use an electric hand mixer to beat until soft and creamy. Add the icing sugar, vanilla and salt and beat for 2–3 minutes or until light. Add the cream cheese and beat briefly just until a smooth buttercream is formed. Spoon or pipe the buttercream onto the base of half the cookies and sandwich with a second. Allow the cookies to rest for a few hours before serving, the cream cheese filling will slightly soften the cookies as they sit, making these cookies beautifully soft and tender.

Stored in the refrigerator, the assembled cookies will keep for up to 5 days. Straight from the refrigerator the cookies can be a little firm so allow them to come to room temperature before enjoying.

Cinnamon Crisp Ice Cream Sandwiches (V)

MAKES 3

These simple cookies utilise leftover scraps of puff pastry and can be adapted no matter how much pastry you have. Based on the French arlette cookie, they are light and crisp and perfect for anyone who loves cinnamon. I like to serve them as sandwich cookies filled with coffee ice cream. Most supermarket puff pastry is made with oil, instead of butter, which means these are also vegan.

125g (4½oz) leftover puff pastry

50g (1¾oz/¼ cup) caster (superfine or granulated) sugar

½ teaspoon ground cinnamon

Pinch of fine sea salt

Preheat the oven to 180°C (160°C Fan) 350°F, Gas Mark 4 and line a baking tray (sheet pan) with parchment paper.

If the pastry you have left over was from a block of homemade or shop-bought pastry, roll it out into a rectangle roughly 24 × 12cm (9½ × 4½in). If using leftover ready-rolled puff pastry, trim your offcut to roughly the same size. Each cookie utilises a 2cm (¾in) wide strip of pastry, so you can easily change how many cookies this recipe makes simply by adding extra pastry and an equivalent amount of sugar.

Mix together the sugar, cinnamon and salt and spread half of it over the piece of puff pastry. Use your hand to gently press the sugar into the pastry, helping to adhere the two together. Roll up the pastry so you end up with a 12cm (4½in) long log.

Use a sharp knife to cut the log into 6 equal discs. Sprinkle the remaining sugar onto a work surface and, working with one piece of pastry at a time, press both cut ends into the sugar and roll out into a circle just over 9cm (3½in) in diameter. Use a 9cm (3½in) round cookie cutter to cut into a neat circle and place on the prepared baking tray.

Sprinkle the cookies with any leftover sugar and then bake for about 25 minutes, or until golden brown. If you flip over the cookies, the sugar should have caramelized and the cookie should resemble the burnished top of a crème brûlée. Remove and set aside until fully cooled.

These cookies are best served on the day they are made. To turn them into ice cream sandwiches, simply sandwich 2 cookies together with a scoop of ice cream; these are particularly good with coffee ice cream.

CHOCOLATE HEAVEN

Reverse Chocolate Chip Cookies

MAKES 6

Take a classic chocolate chip cookie and turn it inside out. The cookie dough is dark and chocolatey, filled with chunks of white chocolate which magically start to caramelize as the cookies bake, adding a real depth of flavour. Inspired by a cookie served at Detroit's Sister Pie, these are a fun take on the classic American chocolate chip cookie.

45g (1½oz/⅓ cup) plain (all-purpose) flour

15g (½oz/3 tablespoons) cocoa powder

¼ teaspoon baking powder

¼ teaspoon bicarbonate of soda (baking soda)

¼ teaspoon fine sea salt

50g (1¾oz/3½ tablespoons) unsalted butter, at room temperature

30g (1oz/2½ tablespoons) caster (superfine or granulated) sugar

30g (1oz/2 tablespoons) light brown sugar

2 large egg yolks

55g (2oz) dark chocolate (65-75% cocoa solids), melted and cooled

50g (1¾oz) white chocolate, roughly chopped

Flaked sea salt, for sprinkling

To make the cookie dough, mix together the flour, cocoa powder, baking powder, bicarbonate soda and salt. In a separate bowl, using an electric hand mixer, beat together the butter and sugars until light and fluffy. Add the egg yolks, one at a time, beating until fully combined before adding the second. Scrape in the melted dark chocolate and mix until evenly combined. Add the flour mixture and mix to form a soft dough. Add the white chocolate and mix briefly to distribute evenly.

The finished cookie dough will be a little soft so, to make it easier to handle, scrape it into a piece of clingfilm (plastic wrap) or a reusable alternative, wrap it up and roll into a roughly 12cm (4½in) long log. Refrigerate for about 1 hour, or until firm.

Preheat the oven to 180°C (160°C Fan) 350°F, Gas Mark 4 and line a large baking tray (sheet pan) with parchment paper.

Remove the cookie dough from the refrigerator and, using a sharp knife, cut the log into 6 equal slices. Place the cookies onto the prepared baking tray, setting them at least 5cm (2in) apart to allow for spreading. Sprinkle with a little flaked sea salt.

Bake for 15-16 minutes. The cookies will be soft when they come out of the oven but will firm up as they cool. Leave to cool for 5 minutes before transferring to wire rack to cool completely.

If stored in a sealed container, these cookies will keep for 3-4 days.

NOTE   I like to make these with black cocoa for an intense black and white colour but any Dutched cocoa powder will work.

Vegan Olive Oil Wholemeal Chocolate Chip Cookies For Two (V)

MAKES 2

My aim with any vegan recipe is to make the end result indistinguishable from the non-vegan version and these smash that out of the park! No one would ever guess they are vegan; the mix of olive oil and wholemeal flour gives the cookies a huge boost of flavour. It is great to have a vegan cookie recipe on hand, but this recipe is also incredibly useful for when you want to make a quick cookie with ingredients that you'll almost definitely have in stock.

30ml (2 tablespoons) olive oil

60g (2¼oz/heaped ¼ cup) light brown sugar

15ml (1 tablespoon) soy milk (or other plant-based milk)

30g (1oz/¼ cup) wholemeal plain (all-purpose) flour

30g (1oz/¼ cup) plain (all-purpose) flour

⅛ teaspoon baking powder

⅛ teaspoon bicarbonate of soda (baking soda)

⅛ teaspoon fine sea salt

30g (1oz) vegan dark chocolate, roughly chopped

Preheat the oven to 180°C (160°C Fan) 350°F, Gas Mark 4 and line a small baking tray (sheet pan) with parchment paper.

Add the oil, sugar and soy milk to a small bowl and mix together to combine. Add the flours, baking powder, bicarbonate of soda and salt and mix to form a dough. Finally, add the chocolate and mix together just until evenly distributed. The finished dough should be soft but not sticky; if needed, mix in a little extra flour to get the correct texture.

Depending on the texture you want from your cookies, you can bake them immediately or wait for 30 minutes and refrigerate them first. The resting time allows the flour to hydrate, resulting in a slightly thicker and chewier cookie.

When ready to bake, divide the dough in half, then roll into balls and place on the prepared baking tray, setting well apart to prevent the cookies from spreading into each other as they bake. Bake for about 16 minutes, or until the edges of the cookies are golden but the centres still a little pale. Remove the baking tray and allow the cookies to cool for 5 minutes before transferring to a wire rack to cool completely.

Stored in a sealed container these cookies will keep for 2–3 days.

Double Brown Butter White Chocolate Macadamia Cookies

MAKES 5

White chocolate macadamia cookies are a classic; the creaminess of the nuts goes perfectly with the white chocolate. This version takes those classic component parts and amps up the flavour. The butter is browned and, as it cooks, milk powder is added, which doubles the level of browned milk solids, massively boosting the flavour. The macadamias are also toasted, adding to the toasty notes in this traditionally very sweet cookie. The cookie is made with a mix of plain flour and cornflour, which helps to create a dense and chewy cookie.

50g (1¾oz/scant ½ cup) macadamia nuts

75g (2½oz/⅔ stick) unsalted butter, diced

1 tablespoon skimmed milk powder (non-fat powdered milk)

85g (3oz/¼ cup + 2 tablespoons) light brown sugar

2½ tablespoons whole milk

85g (3oz/⅔ cup) plain (all-purpose) flour

25g (1oz/3 tablespoons) cornflour (cornstarch)

¼ teaspoon baking powder

⅛ teaspoon fine sea salt

50g (1¾oz) white chocolate, roughly chopped, plus extra (optional), melted, to decorate

---

Before you make the cookies, you need to toast the macadamias. Preheat the oven to 160ºC (140ºC Fan) 325ºF, Gas Mark 3 and scatter the nuts on a rimmed baking tray. Toast the nuts for about 10 minutes, or until golden. You need to keep a close eye when toasting macadamias as they can catch and burn the second you turn your back on them. Remove from the oven and set aside until cool.

Increase the oven temperature to 180ºC (160ºC Fan) 350ºF, Gas Mark 4 and line a baking tray (sheet pan) with parchment paper. Add the butter and milk powder to a small saucepan and cook over a medium heat, stirring constantly, until the butter has melted. As you continue to cook, the butter will splatter as the water cooks out. When it settles and starts to foam, watch out for the milk solids to turn a golden brown. Once golden, pour the butter into a mixing bowl with the sugar and stir to combine. Pour in the milk, stir to combine and set aside for 10 minutes to allow the butter to cool. Add the flour, cornflour, baking powder and salt and mix together until a soft cookie dough is formed. Roughly chop the macadamias and add both the nuts and chocolate to the cookie dough, mixing until evenly distributed.

Roll the cookies into 5 equal balls and place on the prepared baking tray. Bake for 15–16 minutes, or until the cookies are set and the edges are golden. Remove from the oven and allow to cool for 5 minutes before transferring to a wire rack to cool completely. Drizzle melted chocolate over them if you like.

If stored in a sealed container, these cookies will keep for 3–4 days.

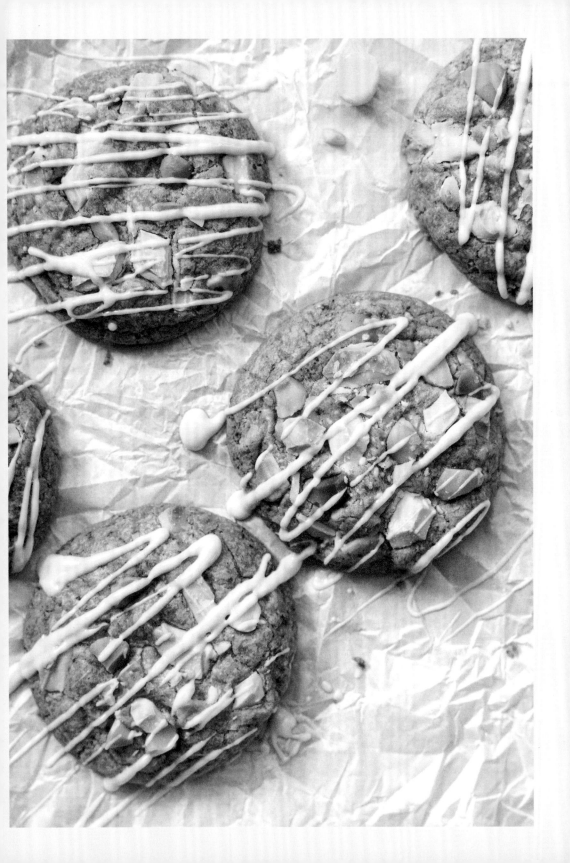

Small Batch Chocolate and Prune Rugelach

MAKES 6

Rugelach are a mainstay of Jewish bakeries; originating in Eastern Europe, their popularity has grown and they can now be found in Jewish communities worldwide. There are two broad categories of rugelach (little twists): those made with a yeasted dough and those made with a cream cheese dough. My version falls into the latter category and are filled with a delightful combination of chocolate and prune. The prunes have a rich fudgy flavour with an almost molasses-like tang, which pairs brilliantly with chocolate.

125g (4½oz/1 cup) plain (all-purpose) flour, plus extra for dusting

Pinch of fine sea salt

30g (1oz/2 tablespoons) unsalted butter, diced and chilled

30g (1oz/2 tablespoons) cream cheese, chilled

3 tablespoons whole milk

FOR THE FILLING

60g (2¼oz) dark chocolate, finely chopped

2 teaspoons cocoa powder

1 tablespoon light brown sugar

Good pinch of fine sea salt

35g (1¼oz/¼ cup) finely diced pitted prunes

FOR THE TOPPING

1 large egg, lightly beaten

Demerara (turbinado) sugar

In a mixing bowl, combine the flour and salt and mix together. Add the butter and use your hands to rub it into the flour until a coarse texture is formed, with some small flakes of butter still present. Add the cream cheese and use a table knife to cut it into the flour mixture. Once the cream cheese is broken into small chunks, use your hands to continue rubbing it into the flour mixture. The finished mixture should resemble coarse breadcrumbs. Drizzle in the milk and use your knife to stir together, forming a shaggy crumbly dough. If the dough holds together when squeezed, no additional moisture is needed; if it is still dry and crumbly, then drizzle in a little extra milk.

Tip the dough onto a lightly floured work surface and use your hands to bring it together into a uniform dough. Form the dough into a rough square, wrap in clingfilm (plastic wrap) or a reusable alternative and refrigerate for 1 hour, or until firm.

Preheat the oven to 180°C (160°C Fan) 350°F, Gas Mark 4 and line a baking tray (sheet pan) with parchment paper.

On a lightly floured work surface, roll out the dough into a 13 × 9cm (5 × 3½in) rectangle. In a small bowl, mix together the chocolate, cocoa powder, sugar and salt. Spread this powdery mixture over the entire surface of the dough. Scatter the prunes over the chocolate mixture. Roll up the dough, from a short edge, into a log, then cut into 6 equal pieces. Brush each rugelach with the beaten egg and sprinkle generously with demerara sugar.

Place the rugelach on the prepared baking tray and bake for 25–30 minutes, or until the pastry is a rich golden brown. Remove and set aside to cool.

If stored in a sealed container, these will keep for 2–3 days but the cookies are at their crispest on the day they are baked.

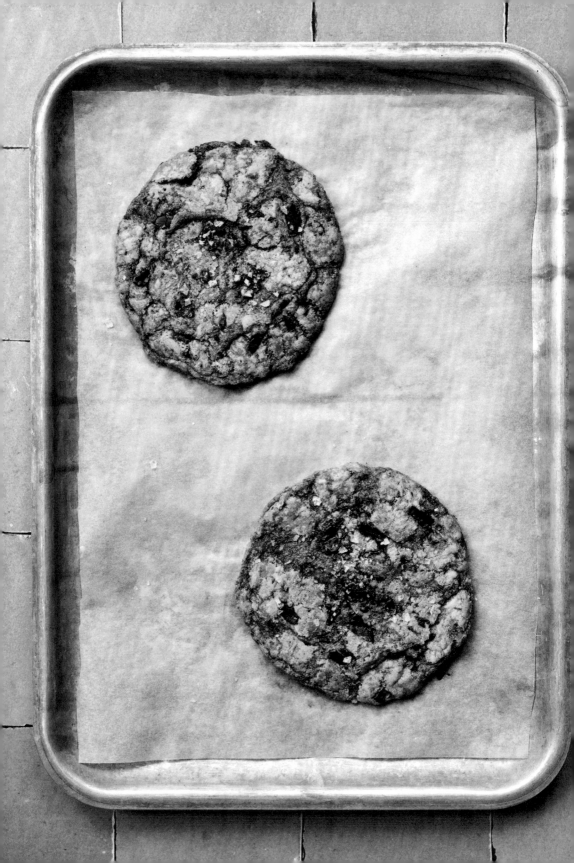

Giant Thin and Crispy Brown Butter Chocolate Chip Cookies

MAKES 2

I have to admit, this cookie completely won me over. I was a crisp chocolate chip cookie sceptic. I always preferred the classic, slightly thick cookie with a crisp edge and a rich chewy centre with plenty of melted chocolate, but these cookies are something special. Because they're baked for longer, to ensure they're crisp all the way through, they caramelize to give a deeply toasty flavour and the crisp texture is a light crackle – they're ridiculously good.

30g (1oz/2 tablespoons) unsalted butter, diced

15g (½oz/1 tablespoon) light brown sugar

35g (1¼oz/3 tablespoons) caster (superfine or granulated) sugar

1 tablespoon whole milk

50g (1¾oz/⅓ cup + 1 tablespoon) plain (all-purpose) flour

⅛ teaspoon baking powder

⅛ teaspoon bicarbonate of soda (baking soda)

⅛ teaspoon fine sea salt

30g (1oz) dark chocolate, roughly chopped

Preheat the oven to 180ºC (160ºC Fan) 350ºF, Gas Mark 4 and line a baking tray (sheet pan) with parchment paper.

Add the butter to a small saucepan, place over a medium heat and cook until browned. The butter will first melt and then start to splutter, as the water content cooks out, then it will foam. It is at this point you should watch for brown flecks to appear in the butter; once they do, the butter is browned.

Pour the butter into a small bowl with the two sugars, mixing together. Add the milk and whisk together until smooth. Add the flour, baking powder, bicarbonate of soda and salt and mix together until a smooth dough is formed. Add the chocolate and mix briefly, just until distributed.

Form the dough into 2 even pieces and roll into balls. Place on the prepared baking tray and bake for about 20 minutes, or until the cookies are golden. Remove the tray from the oven and allow to cool.

These cookies will keep for 2–3 days stored in a sealed container.

Ultimate Vegan Chocolate Chip Cookies (V)

MAKES 6

This is, without a shadow of a doubt, the best vegan chocolate chip cookie I have ever made or tasted. Modelled on my all-time favourite, non-vegan, cookie recipe, it manages to have the perfect texture, a crisp edge and a fudgy centre, and tastes just as good as any other non-vegan chocolate chip cookie. The recipe makes big, bakery-style cookies and they are absolutely jam-packed with chocolate.

100g (3½oz/⅓ cup + 1½ tablespoons) vegan block butter, at room temperature

165g (5¾oz/¾ cup) light brown sugar

3 tablespoons soy milk (or any other plant-based milk)

½ teaspoon vanilla extract

100g (3½oz/¾ cup + 1 tablespoon) plain (all-purpose) flour

100g (3½oz/¾ cup + 1 tablespoon) strong white bread flour

½ teaspoon baking powder

½ teaspoon bicarbonate of soda (baking soda)

½ teaspoon fine sea salt

125g (4½oz) vegan dark chocolate, roughly chopped, plus extra (optional), chopped, to decorate

Flaked sea salt, for sprinkling

In a large bowl, using an electric hand mixer, cream together the vegan butter and sugar, beating for 2–3 minutes or until light and creamy. Add the soy milk and vanilla and mix until fully combined. In a separate bowl, whisk together the flours, baking powder, bicarbonate of soda and salt. Add the flour mixture to the butter mixture and mix, on low speed, just until a uniform dough is formed. Add the chocolate and mix in briefly, just until evenly distributed. Cover the bowl with clingfilm (plastic wrap) or a reusable alternative and refrigerate for at least 1 hour, but preferably overnight, until firm. Chilling the cookies allows the flour to hydrate, giving the perfect end texture.

Preheat the oven to 180°C (160°C Fan) 350°F, Gas Mark 4 and line a baking tray (sheet pan) with parchment paper.

Divide the dough into 6 equal pieces and roll each one into a ball. Place on the prepared baking tray and sprinkle a little flaked sea salt onto each one. You can also press a little extra chocolate onto the outside of the cookie dough balls at this stage if you like – it will give a bakery-quality look to the cookies, as they will have lots of melted chocolate showing on the outside of the cookie.

Bake for about 16 minutes, or until the cookies are golden around the edges and still a little pale in the centres. Remove from the oven and set aside to cool.

If stored in a sealed container, these cookies will keep for 2–3 days.

Chocolate Coffee Crunch Cookies

MAKES 6

When making a traditionally large batch of cookies, the freezer inevitably becomes my friend, as I rarely need the whole batch in one go. Instead, I bake what I need and freeze the rest as balls of cookie dough, ready to bake at a moment's notice. With this small batch recipe, the size isn't an issue, but I still often freeze the whole log of dough after making it, so I always have something in my freezer, ready to bake, when friends come over. These crisp chocolate cookies are fabulous as is, but the added coffee white chocolate coating adds a whole other layer of flavour.

30g (1oz/¼ cup) plain (all-purpose) flour

30g (1oz/¼ cup) wholemeal rye flour

10g (¼oz/2 tablespoons) cocoa powder

¼ teaspoon bicarbonate of soda (baking soda)

Pinch of fine sea salt

50g (1¾oz/3½ tablespoons) unsalted butter, at room temperature

25g (1oz/⅛ cup) caster (superfine or granulated) sugar

25g (1oz/2 tablespoons) light brown sugar

50g (1¾oz) dark chocolate, roughly chopped

FOR THE WHITE CHOCOLATE GLAZE

50g (1¾oz) white chocolate, melted

¼ teaspoon instant espresso powder

To make the cookie dough, sift the flours, cocoa powder, bicarbonate of soda and salt into a bowl and whisk briefly to combine. In a separate bowl, combine the butter and sugars and use an electric hand mixer to beat together for 2–3 minutes, or until pale and creamy. It is important you start with room temperature butter and mix until you have a very creamy-looking mixture; if not, the dough will end up dry and hard to work with. Add the flour mixture to the butter mixture and mix, on low speed, until a crumbly dough is formed. The mixture will start off looking grey but once the flour is fully incorporated, the mixture will darken, forming small chunks of dough that will hold together when pressed together. This is when you want to stop mixing. Add the chocolate and mix very briefly, just until the chocolate is distributed.

Tip the crumbly dough onto a work surface and use your hands to bring together into a uniform dough. Form the dough into a log about 5cm (2in) in diameter. Wrap in clingfilm (plastic wrap) or a reusable alternative and refrigerate for at least 1 hour. At this point you can also freeze the dough for up to 3 months.

Preheat the oven to 180ºC (160ºC Fan) 350ºF, Gas Mark 4 and line a baking tray (sheet pan) with parchment paper.

Remove the dough from the refrigerator and, using a sharp knife, slice into 6 cookies. If the cookies crumble as they're cut, simply press them back together. Place on the prepared baking tray and bake for about 12 minutes, or until the edges are set. Remove and set aside to cool.

For the white chocolate glaze, add the espresso powder to the melted white chocolate and stir to combine. Dip the base of each cookie into the chocolate and set back onto the parchment-lined baking tray. Drizzle any leftover chocolate over the cookies, then refrigerate the cookies until the chocolate is set.

If stored in a sealed container they will keep for 2–3 days.

Peanut Butter Cup Cookies

MAKES 6

These terrific cookies are inspired by one of the all-time greats: the peanut butter cup. The chocolate coating has been replaced by a chewy and dense chocolate cookie but, at their heart, like the classic candy, is a generous peanut butter filling.

75g (2½oz/⅓ cup) unsalted butter, diced, plus extra for greasing

100g (3½oz/⅓ cup + 2 tablespoons) light brown sugar

1 large egg yolk

½ teaspoon vanilla extract

35g (1¼oz/⅓ cup + 2 tablespoons) cocoa powder

75g (2½oz/½ cup + 1½ tablespoons) plain (all-purpose) flour

¼ teaspoon baking powder

¼ teaspoon bicarbonate of soda (baking soda)

¼ teaspoon fine sea salt

30g (1oz) dark chocolate, roughly chopped

Flaked sea salt, for sprinkling (optional)

FOR THE PEANUT BUTTER FILLING

85g (3oz/⅓ cup) smooth peanut butter

40g (1½oz/⅓ cup) icing (powdered) sugar

Pinch of fine sea salt

For the cookie dough, melt the butter either in a small pan set over a low heat or using a microwave. Once melted, pour into a large bowl along with the brown sugar and mix to combine. Once just slightly warm, add the egg yolk and vanilla and mix until smooth.

Sift in the cocoa powder, flour, baking powder, bicarbonate of soda and salt, mixing with a spatula until a cookie dough is formed. Cover with clingfilm (plastic wrap) or a reusable alternative and refrigerate for 30 minutes, or until firm.

While the dough is chilling, prepare the filling. Add the peanut butter, icing sugar and salt to a large bowl and use a spatula to mix together to form a paste.

To assemble the cookies, lightly grease a non-stick muffin tray and preheat the oven to 180°C (160°C Fan) 350°F, Gas Mark 4. Divide the filling into 6 equal pieces and roll each one into a ball. Repeat with the cookie dough. Working with one piece of cookie dough at a time, press into a thin flat disc and place a ball of the filling in the centre. Fold the cookie dough over the filling and press it together to seal. Place the cookie dough in your prepared muffin tray and gently press to slightly flatten it. Repeat with the remaining filling and cookie dough.

Scatter the chopped chocolate on top of the cookies and gently press to adhere the chocolate to the cookies. If you like things that are sweet and salty, I wholeheartedly recommend sprinkling the cookies with a little flaked sea salt at this point as well.

Bake for 15–16 minutes – the cookies will have slightly puffed tops but will still feel a little soft. Remove from the oven and set aside for 20 minutes to cool before carefully turning out from the tray.

If stored in a sealed container, these cookies will keep for 2–3 days.

Grown-up Crispy Puffed Rice Cookies

MAKES 6

As kids, we all loved chocolate rice crispy cakes, or cornflake cakes, right? Sweet and crunchy – what wasn't to like? These incredibly easy cornflake cookies are the grown-up version, the cookie that takes you back to your childhood birthday party. The cookie element is puffed rice cereal mixed with chocolate, which is then filled with a caramelized white chocolate ganache.

40g (1½oz/1½ cups) puffed rice cereal

85g (3oz) milk chocolate, roughly chopped

Pinch of fine sea salt

FOR THE FILLING

100g (3½oz) caramelized white chocolate, finely chopped

3 tablespoons double (heavy) cream

Line a baking tray (sheet pan) with parchment paper and pour the cereal into a large bowl.

Melt the chocolate in either a bowl set over a pan of simmering water or using a microwave in short bursts. Pour the chocolate into the bowl of cereal and stir together until the cereal is evenly coated. Place a 6cm (2½in) round cookie cutter on your prepared baking tray and spoon a little of the cereal mixture into the cutter, using a spoon to compact the cereal mixture into a small puck. To make this process smooth and efficient, I like to spray a little oil onto the inside of the cutter, so none of the cereal mixture sticks when the cutter is removed. Lift away the cookie cutter and repeat to make a total of 12 cookies. Place the baking tray in the refrigerator for 1 hour, or until the chocolate is fully set.

For the filling, melt the chocolate and cream together, either in a bowl set over a pan of simmering water or using a microwave in short bursts. Stir together until a smooth ganache is formed. Set aside until thick but spreadable.

To assemble, peel the cookies from the parchment and spoon a little ganache onto the base of half of the cookies, then sandwich with a second cookie.

If stored in the refrigerator, these cookies will keep for 3–4 days.

NOTE   If you require these to be gluten-free, make sure you check the rice cereal is labelled gluten free, as not all are.

Coconut, Milk Chocolate and Cranberry Cookies

MAKES 6

If you're a fan of any of the popular coconut-based candy bars you will love this recipe, plus you'll find a friend in me, a fellow coconut fan. If you don't like coconut, I won't be entertaining any substitutions – the world is full of coconut-free cookie recipes; let us have this one recipe, one that revels in an abundance of coconut. A chewy cookie packed full of coconut, dried cranberries and milk chocolate, this is a delicious twist on a classic chocolate chip cookie, but to make them extra special, I like to dip the base of the cookie in melted chocolate and then cover the chocolate with even more coconut. I told you this was for coconut lovers.

65g (2¼oz/¼ cup + 1 teaspoon) unsalted butter, at room temperature

110g (3¾oz/½ cup) light brown sugar

3 tablespoons whole milk

80g (2¾oz/⅔ cup) plain (all-purpose) flour

80g (2¾oz/⅔ cup) strong white bread flour

½ teaspoon baking powder

½ teaspoon bicarbonate of soda (baking soda)

½ teaspoon fine sea salt

50g (1¾oz) milk chocolate, roughly chopped

50g (1¾oz/heaped ⅓ cup) dried cranberries

50g (1¾oz/scant ⅔ cup) desiccated (dried shredded) coconut

FOR THE COATING

80g (2¾oz) milk chocolate, melted

50g (1¾oz/scant ⅔ cup) desiccated (dried shredded) coconut

In a large bowl, using an electric hand mixer, beat together the butter and sugar until light and fluffy, about 5 minutes. Don't undermix at this stage – you want a very light mixture. Add the milk, a little bit at a time, beating until fully combined before adding any more. In a separate bowl, whisk together the flours, baking powder, bicarbonate of soda and salt. Add the flour mixture to the butter mixture and mix together until a dough is formed. Add the milk chocolate, cranberries and coconut and mix until evenly distributed. Cover the bowl with clingfilm (plastic wrap) or a reusable alternative and refrigerate for at least 1 hour before baking.

Preheat the oven to 180°C (160°C Fan) 350°F, Gas Mark 4 and line a baking tray (sheet pan) with parchment paper.

Divide the cookie dough into 6 equal pieces and roll each one into a ball. Place on the prepared baking tray, setting them well apart to account for spreading. Bake for 15–16 minutes, or until the edges of the cookies are lightly browned. Remove and set aside for 10 minutes before transferring to a wire rack to cool completely.

Once the cookies are fully cooled, dip the bottom of the cookies into the milk chocolate before dipping into the coconut, so the entire base of the cookie is coated in coconut. Place back on the parchment-lined baking tray and set aside until the chocolate is set.

If stored in a sealed container, in a cool place, these cookies will keep for 3–4 days.

Matcha White Chocolate Chip Cookies

MAKES 6

These cookies have a crisp chewy edge and a soft centre. Made with matcha and white chocolate, they are a match(a) made in heaven – the sweet and buttery white chocolate balances out the grassy and earthy matcha. Made from finely ground green tea leaves, matcha comes in a variety of grades, with ceremonial being the highest and ingredient being the lowest. For baking, I generally use culinary grade, which is a little cheaper than ceremonial but still with great flavour and colour.

60g (2¼oz/¼ cup) unsalted butter, at room temperature

40g (1½oz/3½ tablespoons) caster (superfine or granulated) sugar

40g (1½oz/3½ tablespoons) light brown sugar

1 tablespoon matcha powder (I use culinary grade)

1 large egg

¼ teaspoon vanilla bean paste

125g (4½oz/1 cup) plain (all-purpose) flour

¼ teaspoon bicarbonate of soda (baking soda)

⅛ teaspoon baking powder

¼ teaspoon fine sea salt

50g (1¾oz) white chocolate, roughly chopped

Put the butter and sugars into a bowl and cream together with an electric hand mixer for about 5 minutes, or until light and fluffy. Add the matcha, egg and vanilla and beat until fully combined. Add the flour, bicarbonate of soda, baking powder and salt and mix until an evenly mixed cookie dough is formed. Add the chocolate and mix briefly just until evenly distributed. Cover the cookie dough with clingfilm (plastic wrap) or a reusable alternative and refrigerate for 1 hour before baking.

Preheat the oven to 180°C (160°C fan) 350°F, Gas Mark 4 and line a baking tray (sheet pan) with parchment paper.

Divide the cookie dough into 6 equal pieces and roll each one into a ball. Set onto the prepared baking tray 5cm (2in) apart to account for spreading. Bake for 14–15 minutes, or until the edges of the cookies are just lightly browned. Allow the cookies to cool on the baking tray for 5 minutes before transferring to a wire rack to cool completely.

If stored in a sealed container, these cookies will keep for 3–4 days.

Toasty Malty Milk Chocolate Chunk Cookies

MAKES 2

When people daydream of relaxing by a roaring fire, this is the cookie they should picture eating at the same time. Made with toasted flour and malted milk powder, it's about as toasty and as comforting as it gets. You can mix through any type of chocolate you'd like, but milk chocolate works particularly well here, especially a 'dark milk' chocolate made with a higher than usual cocoa content (around 50% cocoa solids).

35g (1¼oz/2½ tablespoons) unsalted butter, diced

55g (2oz/¼ cup) light brown sugar

2 tablespoons whole milk

2 tablespoons malted milk powder

35g (1¼oz/¼ cup + ½ tablespoon) toasted plain (all-purpose) flour (see page 108)

35g (1¼oz/¼ cup + ½ tablespoon) strong white bread flour

¼ teaspoon baking powder

¼ teaspoon bicarbonate of soda (baking soda)

¼ teaspoon fine sea salt

50g (1¾oz) milk chocolate, roughly chopped

Flaked sea salt, for sprinkling

Using either a small saucepan set over a medium heat, or a microwave, melt the butter. Pour the melted butter into a mixing bowl along with the sugar, milk and malted milk powder and mix together until smooth. Add the flours, baking powder, bicarbonate of soda and salt, then mix to form a smooth cookie dough. Add the chocolate and mix briefly just until distributed.

Scrape the dough into a small bowl, cover with clingfilm (plastic wrap) or a reusable alternative and refrigerate for at least 1 hour until firm.

Preheat the oven to 180°C (160°C Fan) 350°F, Gas Mark 4 and line a baking tray (sheet pan) with parchment paper. Divide the dough into 2 equal pieces and roll them into balls. Place on the prepared baking tray, setting them well apart to account for spreading. Sprinkle the cookies with a little flaked sea salt, then bake for about 16 minutes, or until the edges are little browned. Remove and set aside to cool for 5 minutes before transferring to a wire rack to cool completely.

If stored in a sealed container, these cookies will keep for about 3–4 days.

CHEWY

Ugly Delicious Coffee Toffee Cookies (V)

MAKES 4

These are the dictionary definition of ugly delicious, but what they lack in Instagram-worthy good looks, they make up for in taste. The dense chewy cookies are flavoured with a coffee-infused vegan butter, oats and hazelnuts, but to add a whole other layer of flavour and texture, shards of caramel are mixed through the dough. As the cookies bake, the caramel melts and then, once the cookies have cooled, hardens, leaving crisp chunks of bittersweet caramel mixed through the cookies.

50g (1¾oz/¼ cup) caster (superfine or granulated) sugar

50g (1¾oz/3½ tablespoons) unsalted vegan block butter, diced

1 tablespoon finely ground coffee

60g (2¼oz/heaped ¼ cup) light brown sugar

2 tablespoons soy milk (or other plant-based milk)

40g (1½oz/⅓ cup) plain (all-purpose) flour

20g (¾oz/2½ tablespoons) cornflour (cornstarch)

50g (1¾oz/⅔ cup) traditional rolled oats

35g (1¼oz/heaped ¼ cup) roughly chopped hazelnuts

¼ teaspoon baking powder

⅛ teaspoon fine sea salt

First, we need to make some caramel. Line a small baking tray (sheet pan) with parchment paper and set next to your stove. Pour the caster sugar into a small saucepan and place over a medium heat. Cook the sugar until it is melted and caramelized, turning a rich amber colour. Immediately pour the caramel onto the prepared baking tray and tilt the tray so the caramel spreads into a thin layer. Set aside for at least 30 minutes or until the caramel has set hard, like edible glass.

Preheat the oven to 180ºC (160ºC Fan) 350ºF, Gas Mark 4 and line a baking tray (sheet pan) with parchment paper.

Add the vegan butter and coffee to a small saucepan, place over a medium heat and cook until the butter has melted and just started to bubble. Pour the butter into a bowl, then add the brown sugar and soy milk and mix together until smooth. Add the flour, cornflour, oats, hazelnuts, baking powder and salt and mix to form a cookie dough.

Using the back of a spoon, break the caramel into small chunks and shards. Tip the caramel into the cookie dough and stir to distribute. Divide the dough into 4 equal pieces and roll each one into a ball. The sugar shards can be sharp, so be careful when rolling.

Place the cookies on the prepared baking tray and bake for about 16 minutes, or until the edges of the cookies are golden. Remove and set aside until fully cooled. Don't try to move the cookies until cooled, as the caramel needs time to set.

If stored in a sealed container, these cookies will keep for 2–3 days.

NOTE Leaving in the ground coffee won't be to everyone's taste, so you can happily strain it out once the butter is melted. Just ensure you press on the back of the coffee grounds to strain off as much butter as possible.

Citrus Honey Ricciarelli (GF)

MAKES 6

These fabulous little cookies, inspired by the classic Italian ricciarelli from Tuscany, are similar to amaretti but made with honey, orange zest and some candied peel, giving them a distinctly festive flavour. Instead of the classic diamond shape, I like to roll these into small logs, for an especially elegant look. Traditionally served around Christmas, these are wonderful served alongside a glass of sherry or vin santo.

50g (1¾oz/¼ cup) caster (superfine or granulated) sugar

Zest of ½ orange

125g (4½oz/1¼ cups) ground almonds (almond meal)

⅛ teaspoon fine sea salt

1 large egg white

1 tablespoon honey

A couple of drops of almond extract (optional)

35g (1¼oz/¼ cup) candied citrus peel

Icing (powdered) sugar, for coating

In a large bowl, combine the sugar and orange zest and use your fingertips to rub the zest into the sugar until the sugar is damp and fragrant. Add the ground almonds and salt and mix to combine. To a separate bowl, add the egg white, honey and almond extract (if using) and whisk until the egg white is foamy. Scrape the egg white mixture into the bowl with the ground almond mixture and mix to form a stiff dough.

The candied peel is likely to come chopped into small chunks, but I like to run a knife over the peel to make it more of a minced texture, to ensure it is evenly distributed throughout the cookie dough, so it is in every bite. Add the peel to the dough and mix until evenly distributed. Scrape the dough onto a piece of clingfilm (plastic wrap) or a reusable alternative and form into short sausage shape. Wrap in clingfilm and refrigerate for 4 hours until firm.

Preheat the oven to 180ºC (160ºC Fan) 350ºF, Gas Mark 4 and line a baking tray (sheet pan) with parchment paper.

Remove the ricciarelli dough from the refrigerator and slice into 6 equal pieces. Roll each piece into a short sausage shape, about 6–7cm (2½–2¾in) in length. Roll each one in icing sugar, ensuring the entire cookie is fully coated. Place onto the prepared baking tray and bake for 20–22 minutes, or until the cookies are lightly cracked and lightly browned. Remove and set aside until fully cooled.

If stored in a sealed container, these cookies will keep for up to a week.

Chewy Chocolate and Espresso Cookie

MAKES 1 LARGE COOKIE

Chocolate and coffee – a match made in heaven. The roasted notes of the coffee give the chocolate a boost, a solid backbone, both perfectly accompanied by the rich flavour that comes from using dark brown sugar, packed full of molasses. To make sure both the coffee and the chocolate have their chance to shine, the two are heated together with the butter and milk, allowing the flavours to bloom. When choosing your coffee, you want to use something ground very finely, so the texture of the cookie isn't gritty. And, if your instincts say this would be good with a little chopped chocolate added to the cookie dough, trust your instincts.

20g (¾oz/1½ tablespoons) unsalted butter, diced

25g (1oz/2 tablespoons) dark brown sugar (preferably muscovado)

1 tablespoon whole milk

2 teaspoons cocoa powder

2 teaspoons finely ground coffee

30g (1oz/¼ cup) plain (all-purpose) flour

⅛ teaspoon bicarbonate of soda (baking soda)

⅛ teaspoon fine sea salt

Granulated sugar, for coating

To make the cookie dough, add the butter, sugar, milk, cocoa powder and coffee to a saucepan and, over a low heat, cook until the butter is melted and the mixture just starts to bubble. Immediately pour the butter mixture into a small bowl and set aside to cool to room temperature.

Add the flour, bicarbonate of soda and salt to the butter mixture and use a small spatula to mix together to form a soft cookie dough. Pop the dough into the refrigerator for 20 minutes.

Preheat the oven to 180°C (160°C Fan) 350°F, Gas Mark 4 and line a small baking tray (sheet pan) with parchment paper.

Remove the cookie dough from the refrigerator and roll it into a ball, then roll it in granulated sugar until fully coated. Place the cookie on the prepared baking tray. Bake for 15–16 minutes, or until the edges are set but the centre is puffed and still a little soft. Remove and allow the cookie to cool before enjoying. This is best served on the day made.

NOTE This cookie can easily be made vegan using coconut oil or vegan block butter and any plant-based milk in place of the dairy butter and milk.

Granola Breakfast Cookies (V)

MAKES 4

Crisp edges, chewy centres and jam-packed full of crunchy nuts, these granola cookies are textural heaven. Made from all the component parts used to make granola, there is a whiff of health around these cookies, but don't be fooled, it's nothing more. They're definitely still cookies, albeit slightly less sweet than many others in this book.

50g (1¾oz/⅔ cup) traditional rolled oats

25g (1oz/3 tablespoons) buckwheat flour

35g (1¼oz/¼ cup + 1 teaspoon) wholemeal plain (all-purpose) flour

½ teaspoon ground cinnamon

¼ teaspoon bicarbonate of soda (baking soda)

⅛ teaspoon fine sea salt

50g (1¾oz/3½ tablespoons) coconut oil

25g (1oz/2 tablespoons) light brown sugar

1 tablespoon golden syrup (or maple syrup)

½ tablespoon soy milk (or any other plant-based milk)

25g (1oz/3 tablespoons) raisins

25g (1oz/3 tablespoons) dried cranberries

25g (1oz/scant ¼ cup) roughly chopped toasted hazelnuts

1 tablespoon mixed seeds

Preheat the oven to 180°C (160°C Fan) 350°F, Gas Mark 4 and line a baking tray (sheet pan) with parchment paper.

Add the oats, flours, cinnamon, bicarbonate of soda and salt to a mixing bowl and mix together to combine. In a small saucepan, combine the coconut oil, brown sugar, golden syrup and milk. Place over a low heat and cook, stirring occasionally, until melted and smooth. Pour this mixture into the bowl with the flour mixture and use a wooden spoon to mix together to form a dough. Add the dried fruit, hazelnuts and seeds and mix until evenly distributed. The resulting dough will look a little crumbly but that is as intended.

Divide the dough into 4 equal pieces and use your hands to compress them and roll into balls. Place on the prepared baking tray, setting them well apart to account for spreading. Bake for 15–16 minutes, rotating halfway through baking, or until the edges are browned but the centres are still a little pale. Set aside until fully cooled.

If stored in a sealed container, these cookies will keep for 2–3 days but they will start to soften after the first day, losing their crisp edge.

Anzac Cookies

MAKES 6

These are one of my favourite Antipodean cookies, originally made as part of care packages sent to members of the Australian and New Zealand Army Corps (ANZAC), during the First World War, they are still incredibly popular today. They are one of the easiest cookies to make, are rich and chewy (they can be made to be crunchy too if you prefer) and they last a surprisingly long time.

75g (2½oz/½ cup + 1½ tablespoons) plain (all-purpose) flour

20g (¾oz/¼ cup) desiccated (dried shredded) coconut

50g (1¾oz/⅔ cup) traditional rolled oats

60g (2¼oz/heaped ¼ cup) light brown sugar

30g (1oz/2½ tablespoons) caster (superfine or granulated) sugar

Large pinch of fine sea salt

50g (1¾oz/3½ tablespoons) unsalted butter, diced

20g (¾oz/1 tablespoon) golden syrup or honey

¼ teaspoon bicarbonate of soda (baking soda)

Preheat the oven to 180°C (160°C Fan) 350°F, Gas Mark 4 and line a baking tray (sheet pan) with parchment paper.

In a large bowl, combine the flour, coconut, oats, sugars and salt. Mix together to evenly distribute all of the ingredients. In a small saucepan, combine the butter and golden syrup, place over a low heat and cook until the butter has melted. Remove the pan from the heat and add the bicarbonate of soda and 1 tablespoon of water, mixing together briefly to combine. Pour this mixture into the flour mixture and use a spatula or wooden spoon to mix until evenly combined.

Roll the slightly crumbly dough into 6 equal balls and place them onto the prepared baking tray, setting them 5cm (2in) apart to account for spreading. Bake for 12–15 minutes, or until golden brown around the edges but just a touch paler in the centre. If you want crisp Anzac cookies, you can bake them for an additional 2 minutes. Remove the baking tray from the oven and allow the cookies to cool for 5 minutes before transferring to a wire rack to cool completely.

If stored in a sealed container, these cookies will keep for up to 2 weeks.

NOTE   Golden syrup is the classic ingredient used to make these cookies. If you can't get your hands on any, do not substitute it with corn syrup but use honey instead, which will be a much closer substitution.

Grasmere Gingerbread

MAKES 6

This form of gingerbread, from the beautiful village of Grasmere in the north of the UK, is quite different from anything else you may have had. It may be warming and spicy but it is also chewy and has a crumbly layer on top. Available from just one shop, with the recipe locked away in a safe, far from prying eyes, most people will never have a chance to try it, so this is my humble attempt at replicating it at home. You can make this dough either by hand or using a food processor

50g (1¾oz/3½ tablespoons) unsalted butter, at room temperature, plus extra for greasing

50g (1¾oz/scant ¼ cup) light brown sugar

1 tablespoon black treacle (molasses)

100g (3½oz/⅔ cup + 2 tablespoons) plain (all-purpose) flour

2 teaspoons ground ginger

¼ teaspoon freshly grated nutmeg

Large pinch of fine sea salt

1 tablespoon finely diced crystallized ginger

⅛ teaspoon bicarbonate of soda (baking soda)

Lightly grease a 23 × 13cm (9 × 5in) loaf pan, lining with a single strip of parchment paper so that the excess hangs over the longs sides of the loaf pan, securing in place with a couple metal binder clips.

If making by hand, add the butter, brown sugar and treacle to a mixing bowl and beat together until fully combined. You're not looking to beat in lots of air, simply combine all three ingredients together. Add all the remaining ingredients and mix together with a spatula just to start combining everything together, then use your hands and more of a rubbing motion to form a crumbly dough. Refrigerate the dough for 30 minutes.

Preheat the oven to 180°C (160°C Fan) 350°F, Gas Mark 4.

Remove the bowl from the refrigerator and use your hands to rub into a slightly finer, breadcrumb-like texture. Remove about a third and set aside. Pour the rest of the mixture into the bottom of the prepared loaf pan and use your hands to compress it into an even layer. Sprinkle the remaining mixture on top and leave as a crumbly layer.

If making with a food processor, add the flour, spices, sugar and salt to the bowl of the processor and pulse to combine. Add the butter and treacle and pulse until a crumbly mixture is formed. Add the ginger and pulse briefly to distribute. Once the dough is made, continue as above.

Before baking, use a knife to score the gingerbread into 6 pieces.

Bake for 25–30 minutes, or until a deep golden brown. Remove the pan from the oven and set aside until fully cooled. Use a serrated knife to cut into 6 pieces, using the scored lines as a guide.

If stored in a sealed container, these will keep for at least a week.

Vegan Tahini Oatmeal Chocolate Chip Cookies (V)

MAKES 4

On first glance these may look like any other chocolate chip cookie but that first impression is hiding something different, something with many layers of flavour. The cookie dough is made with tahini, maple syrup and oats but that's not all, the dough is also stuffed with chocolate (of course) and chunks of toasted hazelnuts. The result is a scrumptiously chewy cookie with lots of nuttiness, plus it also happens to be naturally vegan.

75g (2½oz/¼ cup + ½ tablespoon) tahini

1½ tablespoons maple syrup

2 tablespoons soy milk (or other plant-based milk)

30g (1oz/2 tablespoons) light brown sugar

3 tablespoons plain (all-purpose) flour

40g (1½oz/½ cup) traditional rolled oats

¼ teaspoon ground cinnamon

¼ teaspoon fine sea salt

50g (1¾oz) dark chocolate, roughly chopped

50g (1¾oz) toasted hazelnuts, roughly chopped

Flaked sea salt, for sprinkling

Preheat the oven to 180°C (160°C Fan) 350°F, Gas Mark 4 and line a baking tray (sheet pan) with parchment paper.

To make the cookie dough, add the tahini, maple syrup, soy milk and sugar to a small bowl and mix together until smooth. Add the flour, oats, cinnamon and salt and mix together to form a cookie dough. Add the chocolate and hazelnuts and mix until evenly distributed.

Divide the dough into 4 equal pieces and roll each one into a ball. Place the cookies on the prepared baking tray and sprinkle with a little flaked sea salt. If you want an especially enticing cookie you add a little extra chopped chocolate and hazelnuts to the outside of the cookies before baking.

Bake for about 18 minutes, or until the edges are golden. Remove from the oven and give the baking tray a firm tap on the work surface to collapse the cookies slightly, which helps make them extra chewy. Set the cookies aside until cooled.

If stored in a sealed container, these cookies will keep for 2–3 days.

Almond Horns (GF)

MAKES 6

Italy might have amaretti but Germany has mandelhörnchen, an almond paste-based cookie that is dense and chewy with a whisper of chocolate and a whole lot of flaked almonds. A traditional Christmas cookie, found at Christmas markets across the country, these work best made with almond paste as opposed to marzipan. The latter has less almond and more sugar, which means the cookies wouldn't hold their shape as well, and the texture would be softer and the taste sweeter. They keep exceptionally well, so are great make-ahead Christmas gifts.

115g (4oz) almond paste (50% almond content)

50g (1¾oz/¼ cup) caster (superfine or granulated) sugar

50g (1¾oz/½ cup) ground almonds (almond meal)

1 large egg white

¼ teaspoon almond extract (optional)

Pinch of fine sea salt

50g (1¾oz/½ cup) flaked almonds

100g (3½oz) dark chocolate, melted

To make the cookie dough, crumble the almond paste into a large bowl, breaking it up into small pieces. Add the sugar and ground almonds and mix together. In a separate bowl, lightly whisk the egg white, then pour half into the almond paste mixture along with the almond extract, if using, setting the other half aside for the moment. Using an electric hand mixer, mix everything together until a stiff but evenly combined mixture is formed. Cover with clingfilm (plastic wrap) or a reusable alternative and refrigerate for 1 hour, or until firm.

Preheat the oven to 180°C (160°C Fan) 350°F, Gas Mark 4 and line a baking tray (sheet pan) with parchment paper. Divide the dough into 6 equal pieces and roll each one into a roughly 15cm (6in) long log, slightly tapering the ends. Using the reserved egg white, paint each cookie all over to make the outside slightly sticky, then coat entirely in the flaked almonds. Bend the cookie into a horseshoe shape and place on the prepared baking tray.

Bake for about 15 minutes, or until the cookies are just lightly golden. Remove and set aside to cool. Once cool enough to handle, dip the ends in the chocolate and set back onto the baking tray. Set aside until the chocolate has set.

If stored in a sealed container in a cool spot, these cookies will keep for up to 2 weeks.

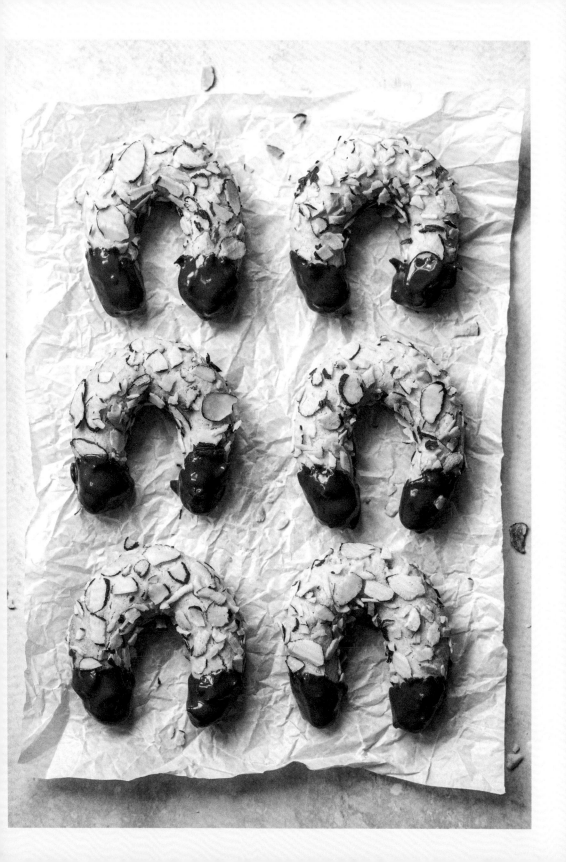

Single Serve Pecan Butterscotch Cookie

MAKES 1 LARGE COOKIE

If you read my last book, you might have come across my 'emergency' cookie – a classic, but single serve, chocolate chip cookie. This new cookie is inspired by that recipe but adapted to make a chewy version studded with crunchy chunks of butterscotch and toasted pecans. If you want to turn this into a dessert, I can wholeheartedly recommend crumbling it over vanilla ice cream.

1 tablespoon unsalted butter, melted and slightly cooled

2 tablespoons light brown sugar

½ tablespoon whole milk

1½ tablespoons plain (all-purpose) flour

1½ tablespoons strong white bread flour

Pinch of baking powder

Pinch of bicarbonate of soda (baking soda)

Pinch of fine sea salt

2 butterscotch candies (I used Werther's Original), roughly chopped

2 tablespoons roughly chopped pecans, lightly toasted

Preheat the oven to 180ºC (160ºC Fan) 350ºF, Gas Mark 4 and line a small baking tray (sheet pan) with parchment paper.

In a small bowl, mix together the butter, sugar and milk until fully combined and smooth. Add the flours, baking powder, bicarbonate of soda and salt and mix to form a cookie dough. Add the butterscotch candies and pecans and mix briefly to distribute.

Form the dough into a ball and place on the prepared baking tray. Bake for about 16 minutes until the edges are golden and the centre still a little pale. Remove and set aside to cool.

Best enjoyed on the day it is made.

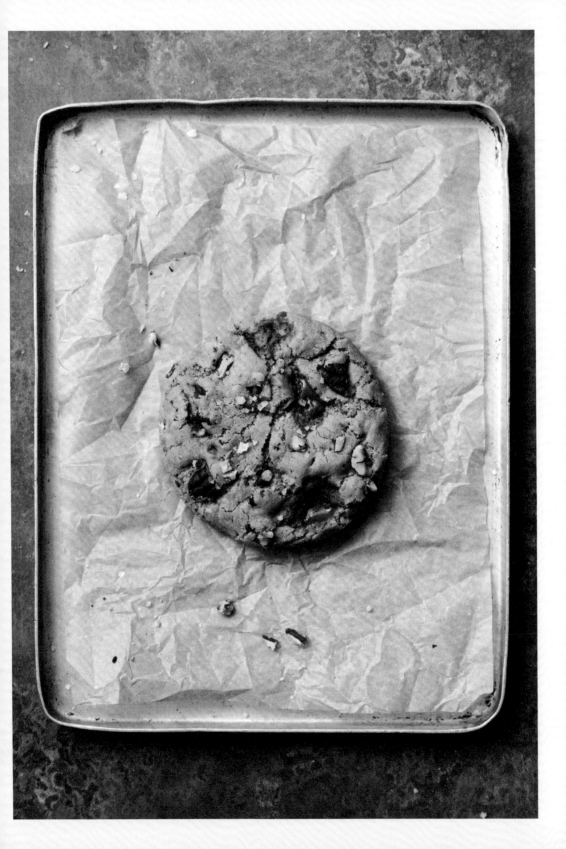

Birthday Cake Ice Cream Sandwiches

MAKES 6

If you're wondering what on earth 'birthday cake' flavour is actually supposed to taste like, I understand your quandary. Seemingly an invention of big food manufacturers in the early 2000s, it has come to mean something vanilla-flavoured with a lot of colourful sprinkles. The flavour is meant to provide you with twangs of nostalgia. To really push home that old-school bakery vibe, I like to sneak a tiny amount of almond extract into the cookie dough, which, to my mind, really amplifies this sense of the old-fashioned.

120g (4¼oz/1 stick + ½ tablespoon) unsalted butter, at room temperature

100g (3½oz/½ cup) caster (superfine or granulated) sugar

50g (1¾oz/scant ¼ cup) light brown sugar

1 large egg

1 teaspoon vanilla bean paste

200g (7oz/1½ cups + 1 tablespoon) plain (all-purpose) flour

2 tablespoons skimmed (non-fat) milk powder

½ teaspoon baking powder

½ teaspoon bicarbonate of soda (baking soda)

½ teaspoon fine sea salt

75g (2½oz) white chocolate chips

100g (3½oz) rainbow sprinkles

Vanilla ice cream, for the filling

To make the cookies, place the butter and sugars into a large bowl and beat together for about 5 minutes, or until light and fluffy. Add the egg and vanilla and beat for a couple minutes, or until fully combined. In a separate bowl, mix together the flour, milk powder, baking powder, bicarbonate of soda and salt. Add the flour mixture to the butter mixture and mix on low speed until a uniform cookie dough is formed. Add the chocolate chips and sprinkles and mix briefly into the dough until distributed. Cover the dough with clingfilm (plastic wrap) or a reusable alternative and refrigerate for at least 1 hour before baking.

Preheat the oven to 180°C (160°C Fan) 350°F, Gas Mark 4 and line a couple baking trays (cookie sheets) with parchment paper.

Divide the cookie dough into 12 equal pieces and roll each one into a ball. Place the cookies on the prepared baking trays and bake for 16–18 minutes, or until golden at the edges and still a touch pale in the centre.

Remove from the oven and give the baking tray a firm tap on the work surface to collapse the cookies slightly and make them even chewier. Set aside for 10 minutes before transferring to a wire rack to cool completely.

To assemble into ice cream sandwiches, flip half of the cookies upside down and top with a scoop of vanilla ice cream. Add a second cookie on top of the ice cream and press to flatten the ice cream so that it almost peeks out from the sides. Place the sandwiches in a sealed container and freeze until ready to enjoy.

If kept frozen, the cookies are good for up to a month.

Hazelnut Crinkle Cookies (GF)

MAKES 6

These are a simple hazelnut variation of the classic Italian amaretti but the flavour change makes them taste like something else entirely. Warm and toasty from the ground hazelnuts (hazelnut meal), you could keep these nice and simple, or if you want to add even more flavour, try mixing through some mini chocolate chips.

1 large egg white

70g (2½oz/¾ cup) ground almonds (almond meal)

70g (2½oz/¾ cup) ground hazelnuts (hazelnut meal)

65g (2¼oz/⅓ cup) caster (superfine or granulated) sugar

Pinch of fine sea salt

½ teaspoon gluten-free baking powder

Icing (powdered) sugar, for coating

In a large bowl, whisk the egg white until foamy. You aren't looking to make meringue with the egg white, but beating it like this helps it combine more easily with the other ingredients. Add the remaining ingredients and mix to form a slightly sticky dough. To make it easier to handle, cover with clingfilm (plastic wrap) or a reusable alternative and refrigerate for 30 minutes–1 hour.

Preheat the oven to 180ºC (160ºC Fan) 350ºF, Gas Mark 4 and line a baking tray (sheet pan) with parchment paper. Fill a small bowl with icing sugar. Divide the dough into 6 equal pieces and roll each one into a ball. Roll each cookie in the icing sugar, lightly compacting the sugar onto the cookie to ensure a generous coating. Place the cookies on the prepared baking tray.

Bake for 17–20 minutes, or until the cookies are cracked and the dough peeking through the icing sugar coating is golden. Remove the baking tray and set aside until the cookies are cooled.

If stored in a sealed container, these cookies will keep for up to 2 weeks.

NOTE If you are baking these for someone with a gluten allergy it is best to check that the baking powder is classified as gluten-free, as due to cross-contamination not all brands are.

Chewy Flourless Double Chocolate Cookies (GF)

MAKES 6

These naturally gluten-free chocolate cookies get a delightful chew from the oat flour, and with their simplicity there is almost something a little retro about them. They taste like something you would have loved as a child, just pure unadulterated chocolate heaven.

75g (2½oz/⅓ cup) unsalted butter, at room temperature

90g (3¼oz/⅓ cup + 1 tablespoon) light brown sugar

1 tablespoon whole milk

½ teaspoon vanilla extract

35g (1¼oz/⅓ cup + 2 tablespoons) cocoa powder

100g (3½oz/1 cup + 2 tablespoons) oat flour

½ teaspoon bicarbonate of soda (baking soda)

¼ teaspoon fine sea salt

100g (3½oz) dark chocolate, roughly chopped

Preheat the oven to 180ºC (160ºC Fan) 350ºF, Gas mark 4 and line a baking tray (sheet pan) with parchment paper.

In a mixing bowl, beat together the butter and sugar until light and fluffy, about 5 minutes. Add the milk and vanilla and beat briefly until fully combined.

In a separate bowl, whisk together the cocoa powder, oat flour, bicarbonate of soda and salt. Add the flour mixture to the butter mixture and mix until a uniform cookie dough is formed. Add the chocolate and mix briefly just until evenly distributed. Divide the dough into 6 equal pieces, then roll each one into a ball. Place the cookies on the prepared baking tray, setting them well apart to account for spreading.

Bake for 15–16 minutes until spread and lightly cracked. The cookies will be soft but will set further as they cool.

If stored in a sealed container, these cookies will keep for 2–3 days.

NOTE   If you want to veganize this recipe, simply switch the butter and milk for vegan alternatives.

About Edd

Edd Kimber is a baker and food writer based in London. He is the author of *The Boy Who Bakes* (2011), *Say It With Cake* (2012), *Patisserie Made Simple* (2014), *One Tin Bakes* (2020), *One Tin Bakes Easy* (2021) and the *Sunday Times* bestselling *Small Batch Bakes* (2022). Over the last ten years he has appeared on multiple television shows including *Good Morning America*, *The Alan Titchmarsh Show*, *Sunday Brunch*, *Saturday Kitchen* and, of course, on the original series of *The Great British Bake Off*, of which he is the inaugural winner. He writes a newsletter on Substack and is a regular contributer to multiple print and digital publications both in the UK and abroad.

@THEBOYWHOBAKES WWW.THEBOYWHOBAKES.CO.UK EDDKIMBER.SUBSTACK.COM

Resources

General Bakeware

- Divertimenti www.divertimenti.co.uk
- Williams Sonoma www.williams-sonoma.com

Eighth Sheet Pan

- Nordicware www.nordicware.com

Flour

- Doves Farm Flour www.dovesfarm.co.uk
- Matthews Cotswold Flour www.cotswoldflour.com
- King Arthur Baking www.kingarthurbaking.com
- Gold Medal Flour www.goldmedalflour.com

Vanilla Products

- Heilala www.heilalavanilla.com

Tahini

- Belazu www.belazu.com
- Seed and Mill www.seedandmill.com

Chocolate

- Guittard www.guittard.com
- Pump Street Chocolate www.pumpstreetchocolate.com
- Islands Chocolate www.islandschocolate.com

Matcha

- Japan Centre www.japancentre.com
- Kenko Matcha www.kenkomatcha.com

Spices

- Rooted Spices www.rootedspices.com
- Burlap and Barrel www.burlapandbarrel.com

Index

Acknowledgements

Thanks to Judith, Isabel, Hazel, Vic, Liz and the whole team at Kyle Books for letting me run free with my ideas, helping me craft them into this brilliant little book and getting that book into stores and people's kitchens. Thanks to Evi and team for the beautiful design direction.

Thanks to Katherine for looking after me for over ten years, I can't quite believe this is book number seven!

Thanks to Mike (and Wesley), Simon and everyone else I have foisted cookies upon and demanded a thorough evaluation from. Thanks for your input and for being a springboard for many delicious ideas.

I have been writing cookbooks for fourteen years and it is not lost on me that this is a very special position to be in, so the biggest thanks goes to everyone who reads my books and bakes my recipes, I will forever strive to bring you bites of deliciousness with recipes you can rely on.

Edd x